A VISUAL JOURNEY THROUGH A BELOVED TEXAS TOWN

Principal Photographer: Kristi Reese, Kristi Reese Photography
Authors: Clint Reese and Kristi Reese
Cover illustration and page design: Kristi Reese

Copyright © 2016 by Kristi Reese. All rights reserved.

No part of this book may be reproduced in any written, electronic, recording, or photocopying form without written permission of the authors and photographer.

Although every precaution has been taken to verify the accuracy of the information contained herein, the author, photographer, and publisher assume no responsibility for any errors or omissions. No liability is assumed for damages that may result from the use of information contained within.

Printed in the United States of America

First printing, 2016

ISBN 13 978-0-692-66842-9
ISBN 10 0-692-66842-X

For a list of retailers or to purchase this book online,
visit www.GrapevineTexasJourney.com or www.KristiReesePhotography.com

thank you

Grapevine holds a special place in my heart. It's where my husband and I met, had our first date, exchanged wedding vows, and started our family. Grapevine is the backdrop of my fondest stories.

The journey of encapsulating this amazing city has been a road I could not have traveled alone. Grapevine's finest residents, artists, business owners, civic leaders, friends, and family helped bring this labor of love to fruition. The true spirit of Grapevine shines through in the ways residents cherish the past, enjoy the present, and envision the future. The heart of the city that can't be put into mere words and pictures is the spirit of the people who each and every day work to make Grapevine a shining jewel in the crown of Texas.

I am indebted to all of you who have helped me along the way. You made my telling of the story interesting, exciting, and inviting. My hope is that I've been able to share your love and passion for Grapevine in the process.

A very special thank you to Clint Reese, Linda Brown, Sallie Andrews, Debi Meek, Sharron Spencer, Paul W. McCallum, William D. Tate, Lindsey Fortin, Eloise Koehn, Grapevine Historical Society, Grapevine High School, Grapevine Convention & Visitors Bureau, and the City of Grapevine.

From the bottom of my heart, thank you. Cheers!

Kristi Reese

Well hello there, friends. It's time to sit back, relax, and enjoy a journey through the beautiful and historic town of Grapevine, Texas.

Grapevine's legacy began in 1843 with Texas hero, Sam Houston. He and representatives of the Republic of Texas met with members of ten American Indian nations to sign a peace treaty at Grape Vine Springs, also known as "Tah-Wah-Karro Creek." The treaty was completed at Birds Fort, and thus named the Treaty at Birds Fort.

The treaty opened North Texas for settlement and that's precisely what happened. Within a year, settlers began arriving via covered wagon along the Grape Vine Prairie. Grapevine is the oldest settlement in Tarrant County; the town originated under the Lone Star flag of the Republic of Texas in 1844, one year before Texas became a state.

In 1854 it came time to make the town official - a name and a post office were the last pieces of the puzzle. A controversy arose with regard to the naming of the town. "Suggsville" and "Dunnville" were contenders for the city's name. Judge Morehead recommended the name "Grape Vine" due to the proximity of Grape Vine Springs, the Grape Vine Prairie, and the sprawling vines of wild mustang grapes growing in excess around the town. Grape Vine won the vote, and in 1914 a change was made by the post office making the town's name a single word, Grapevine.

In the late 1880s, Grapevine was touted as being a wholesome place to live as it had yet to be tainted by the sinful nature of vices such as saloons and billiard halls. Thankfully, someone eventually discovered what all those grapes were for.

From Bonnie and Clyde and unearthed dinosaur remains, to hauntings and world-renowned festivals, Grapevine's history is as full and rich as the wine it produces.

The tintype photo to the left is the oldest known photograph of Grapevine, circa 1856. What follows are photos of historic and history-making events. Tour the beautiful winding history and present of the wonderful city of Grapevine. After all, you don't know where you're going unless you know where you've been.

Welcome, y'all!

1908

1922

1940

2015

1900

1925

2015

In 1888, the St. Louis Southwestern Railway, also known as the Cotton Belt Railroad, reached Grapevine as a stop for travelers between Missouri and Fort Worth. The train was named for the cotton that grew abundantly in the region.

Today, the Grapevine Vintage Railroad is one of Grapevine's most popular attractions, providing a glimpse of travel in the Old West with regular trips to the Fort Worth Stockyards. The train also hosts numerous special events throughout the year.

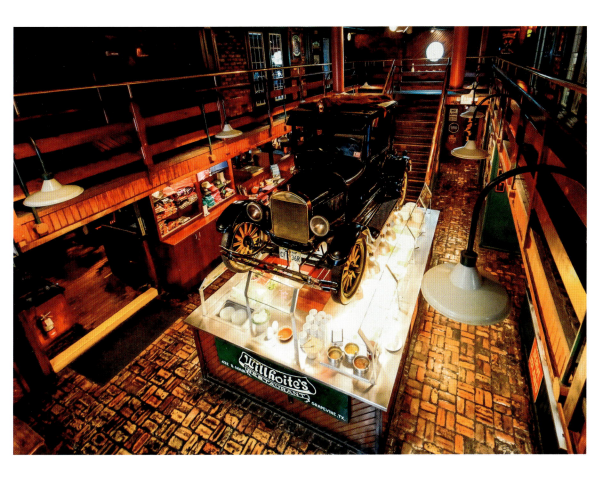

Whether it's fuel for your automobile, or "fuel" for your body, Willhoite's has provided it for more than a century. Built in 1914, this historic building first opened as a dry goods store and theatre. In 1921, it became Willhoite Garage, the first automotive garage in Grapevine, complete with a full service gas station.

In 1981, Willhoite's Restaurant opened, allowing diners to fuel up with spirits and fare. A 1928 Ford Model T is hoisted above the buffet alongside many other historic artifacts about the garage-turned restaurant. Motorcycle enthusiasts have plenty of streetside eye candy to ogle, as patrons regularly arrive to this honky tonk on two wheels.

Constructed circa 1900, this historical gem opened as Grapevine National Bank. Eighteen years later it was renamed Grapevine Home Bank. Grapevine Home Bank became famous in 1932 when it was robbed by J. Les "Red" Stewart and Odell Chambless, both members of the infamous Bonnie and Clyde gang. The bank was held up at gunpoint and bank officials were locked inside the vault. One burglar didn't get very far and was caught the very same day. As luck would have it, he was the one with the getaway car and half of the stolen cash.

Bonnie and Clyde and their posse spent quite a bit of time in Grapevine and surrounding areas. Two years after the Grapevine Home Bank robbery, they shot and killed State Highway Patrolmen E.B. Wheeler and H.D. Murphy on Highway 114 and Dove Road.

Bonnie and Clyde committed over 200 robberies and killed 13 people, including nine law enforcement officers. The couple was tracked by a six-man posse for 102 days, and their vicious reign came to an end on May 23, 1934 when they were ambushed in Louisiana. The 1934 V-8 Ford they were driving was riddled with 167 bullet holes. They were buried in their home town of Dallas, Texas in separate cemeteries.

Today, Bermuda Gold & Silver, a family-owned custom jewelry boutique since 1983, practices "Old World Integrity" in serving customers - their extended family. Patrons who enter through the original Grapevine Home Bank doors will find a bank teller window, framed artifacts, and historic Grapevine photos.

Six Leased Wires Serve The Star-Telegram Exclusively With the Day's News of the World—Associated Press (Four), International News Service, Consolidated Press

MORNING

FORT WORTH STAR-TELEGRAM

A FORT WORTH OWNED NEWSPAPER

CITY EDITION

VOLUME LII. NUMBER 335. FORT WORTH, TEXAS *** *Where the West Begins* ***SATURDAY, DECEMBER 31, 1932. TWELVE PAGES PRICE 5 CENTS

ROBBER TRICKS FARMERS INTO HELPING IN ESCAPE

Today

Washington, Drizzly, Calm.

What, No Sales Tax?

The Baby, Invisible.

By Arthur Brisbane

The Brisbane column is published by The Star-Telegram as a news feature because of the interesting comments of this distinguished writer upon topics of the day. The views expressed are those of Mr. Brisbane and should not be interpreted as reflecting the editorial opinions or policies of this newspaper.—Editor's Note.

Your country grows rapidly. George M. Reynolds announces his retirement as head of the Continental Illinois National Bank because, at 68, he wants "the remaining years of my life to be free from business," and reminds you how rapidly things grow in this country.

"When I came to Chicago in December, 1897 (only 35 years ago), the population was 1,600,000. It is now about 3,600,000. When I came to Chicago, its bank deposits were $380,000,000. They are now more than $3,000,000,000."

He who thinks this little depression can stop such growth as that, for all time, doesn't know his own country.

You have heard it said: "Everything is all right as long as I have my health." Uncle Sam can say that despite the depression, for he has his health.

Mr. Frederick Ecker, head of the Metropolitan Life Company, finds that 1932 has been the healthiest year in our history.

Deaths among Metropolitan policyholders, among whom a large number have borne the brunt of unemployment, were fewer than in any other year. That is partly due to the fact that people have lived more soberly, eating moderately, using less alcohol, and due also to Mr. Ecker's wise policy of advertising widely sound information on how to keep well, and live longer.

The greatest advertisement is the rainbow, full page wide, with colors, put in the heavens to advertise an end of floods. That magnificent advertisement turns out to be a small thing compared with fireworks that exist in space.

Profesor Dugan of Princeton describes a "cosmic pinwheel" made up of two balls of fire, as big as 24 of our suns, whirling in space at the rate of a million miles an hour and it whirls in a space less than 20,000,000 miles wide. Just like the pinwheel you used to fasten to an apple tree.

It is hard to imagine a pinwheel 24 times as big as our sun, because our sun is 1,000,000 times as big as this earth and our little brains can not even imagine the size of the earth.

The Democratic party may reach March 4 with everybody "horrified." Those that know how rapidly a national deficit of $100,000,000 a month

(TURN TO PAGE 2, COLUMN 1)

Rail Commission Speeds Oil Hearing

ORDER MUST BE READY BY TOMORROW

Hunt for Illegally-Produced Crude Will Be Resumed at Tyler on January 12.

Nominations for East Texas Expected to Be Sifted Down to 300,000 Barrels.

BY JOHN W. NAYLOR.
Star-Telegram Oil Editor.

AUSTIN, Dec. 30. — Sidetracking the quest for "hot oil" and other production over allowables in East Texas Friday, the Railroad Commission drove rapidly through testimony on market demand for oil from various Texas oil fields and physical conditions in the field in order to assemble data on which the next proration orders will be based. The change in direction of the inquiry was explained as due to the necessity for the promulgation of new proration orders by Jan. 1, and *not from* any desire to close down on the inquiry into leaks in enforcement of oil regulations.

In fact, the commission announced that it would recess this hearing to Tyler Jan. 12, where the entire time will be devoted to a quest for the illegally produced oil and the way it is taken out of the field. For that purpose more than 50 witnesses, including pipe line officials, railroad officials, purchasers and producers who were subpoenaed to the present hearing were notified to appear in Tyler for questioning. The commission also promised fullest latitude into the inquiry of the activity of its own personnel in the field.

With the turn of the inquiry into more prosaic channels, a good part of the crowd in attendance, the greatest of any recorded at a proration hearing, left Friday afternoon. Additional nominations heard and testimony adduced at Friday's hearing indicated little basis for material changes from present proration schedules. The questioning of witnesses was again marked by a drive on the part of East Texas representatives in an effort to show that older fields were allowed more than their rightful share in the hope of giving more latitude for East Texas production allowances. Apparently this quest ran up against a stone wall in the instance of the Yates and Van areas, which witnesses indicated were as severely prorated, or more so, than East Texas. This repeated experience at former hearings.

It appeared likely Friday that the nominations for East Texas oil would sift down to 300,000 barrels, com-

(TURN TO PAGE 2, COLUMN 3)

Soon After Robbery of Bank by Two Young Bandits

Pictures taken soon after the holdup yesterday of the Grapevine Home Bank. In the upper left photo, Constable Coleman of Grapevine (left) has in custody Les Stewart, who admitted participation in robbery. News of the holdup created great excitement as a view of the crowd in front of the bank shows (upper right). At the lower left, R. E. Morrow (right), bank president, is shown as he appeared, discussing business matters with Frank Crawford, when the two robbers entered. At the lower right are shown S. A. Wall, vice president, (left), Cashier H. C. Yancey (center), and C. H. Holt, trucking contractor, standing at the entrance to the vault, in which they and three others were locked.

—Star-Telegram Photos.

800 Salesmen Get New Jokes, Ideas, Courage At Annual Dinner

Eight hundred salesmen — almost twice the expected attendance—got a sample case full of new jokes, new ideas, new courage and new determination last night.

They laughed off memories of depressed business and left their tenth annual Salesmen's Roundup at The Texas with a resolution to meet 1933 at the front door, take the New Year courteously but firmly by the arm and lead it to a new and profitable state on the business map.

A woman, Miss Alma Cloud, sales manager of a Dallas hosiery firm, told them how.

"Quit buying business with price appeal," was her plea. "Sell merchandise for a profit."

She entered a squared ring that had been arranged for athletic exhibitions, pulled off her hat and let 'em have it straight to the chin in jabs, hooks, uppercuts and knockout blows.

'Too Much Conversation.'

"There has been too much conversation and theorizing about business and the financial situation," she asserted. "The unemployed are not half so big a problem as the unemployable. You've talked in the past about romance in business. But the romance in business now is profits.

"Business is neither a skin game nor a philanthropy—it is selling at a profit," she continued. "The days of miracles have passed. If you're waiting for something to turn up, the only thing turning up will be your toes.

"The hardest thing people have to do nowadays is to meet the competition of bankrupts," she went on. "Bankrupts are content with salvaging anything from their wrecked businesses. But I want to tell you that bankrupts are being eliminated fast.

"In 1933, you've got to look better, talk better and act better than any other salesman. Spend your time working pay dirt only. You've got to know your product and win the confidence of your customer. And remember that making friends is essential. And lastly, you've got to develop an unlimited supply of genuine, high-powered, double-barreled, triple-filtered enthusiasm."

'Victories Are but Taste.'

Amon G. Carter, toastmaster, who served in the same capacity in each preceding roundup, recalled that the first of the events a decade ago was, "first, the noisiest, then the orderliest bunch of fellows that had ever been in Fort Worth."

"The world doesn't like a quitter," he said. "It wants the man who can do a job in spite of everything. The man with spirit, courage, foresight is the man who gets along. There will be opportunities in the coming year for you to do more than ever before for your employes, your employers and for your businesses."

Carter introduced George Kemble, assistant district attorney, who declared in welcoming the group: "You salesmen have not been failures but tremendous successes during 1932. Your victories are but a taste of the triumph that the New Year holds."

C. B. McCaulay, member of the arrangements committee, administered

(TURN TO PAGE 2, COLUMN 8)

ACTS AS LOST POSSEMAN TO GET CAR RIDE

Pistol Drawn After Journey Is Begun; Driver Has to Take Bandit to Dallas.

One of Pair That Held Up Bank at Grapevine Held, Part of Loot Recovered.

BY BOYCE HOUSE.
Staff Correspondent.

GRAPEVINE, Dec. 30.—Kidnaped by a bank robber who knocked at his door and posed as a lost member of a posse searching for the robber, W. A. Shumaker, 37, farmer residing four miles south of here, returned to Grapevine tonight to relate how he was forced at the point of a pistol to drive the robber to the edge of Dallas.

One of the two robbers who fled from the Grapevine Home Bank at noon with $2,850 was captured six miles south of here less than two hours after the holdup and $1,425 was recovered. Under the name of Lee Stewart, 20, he was charged by complaint in Justice Faulkner's Court in Fort Worth with armed robbery.

Wearing mud-splattered clothing, the stranger knocked loudly at Shumaker's back door just after sunset. He explained he came from Dallas with an uncle to join the citizens posse in search for the robber and that he was lost from his group. He asked Shumaker to drive him to Grapevine.

At Shumaker's fireside, the imposter talked in detail of the daring daylight robbery with the family while Shumaker, acting as a "Good Samaritan," prepared his car for the four-mile trip into town.

"The robber was in the house about 10 minutes," Shumaker said. "He talked with Jesse Trigg, my brother-in-law; my wife; Miss Maud Williams and George Conley, hired hand. When he came in his clothing was wet and he told us he had fallen in a creek."

Trigg made the trip with Shumaker and the robber. Half a mile from the house the robber, still posing as a posse member, drew a pistol and ordered Shumaker to drive him to Dallas.

Before getting out of the car and walking away in the edge of Dallas the man admitted to Shumaker and Trigg he was one of the bank robbers.

"I have 58 shells in my pocket," the robber said, "and I intend to use them before they get me."

"I'll get out here," the robber said as he commanded Shumaker to slow down and turn his car around on the Dallas-Northwest Highway in the western suburbs of Dallas. He alighted from the car after the turn was made and disappeared on foot toward Dallas.

Shumaker said the robber appeared to be about 25. He was dressed in

(TURN TO PAGE 2, COLUMN 4)

WILLIAMS PICKS SEVEN DEPUTIES

A "shakeup" in the personnel of the county engineer's office and the appointment of seven deputy tax assessors were announced yesterday as incoming county officials put finishing touches to their plans to take over reins of the courthouse Monday for two-year terms.

A few hours after Wesley Stevens was notified of his reappointment as county engineer, 11 members of his staff were informed they will not be retained after Jan. 1. The appointment of nine or 10 persons to succeed the discharged employes will be made by the new Commissioners Court Monday.

Four members of Stevens' staff will be retained. They are: E. F. McMurtrey, first assistant in charge of construction; W. L. Kelly, bridge engineer, and Matt Walker, chief computer, and F. D. Hughes, bridge designer. The present staff of 17 members will be reduced to 13 or 14. Another reduction in the staff's size

(TURN TO PAGE 2, COLUMN 5)

Bexar County Clerk Found With Throat Cut

By Associated Press.

SAN ANTONIO, Dec. 30—Jack R. Burke, Bexar County clerk, under indictment on a charge of misappropriating public funds, was found seriously wounded tonight alone in a room at a tourist camp here. A sharp kitchen knife was found beside him. His throat had been slashed.

Sheriff Albert Hausser ordered Burke transferred to a hospital as soon as his condition permitted and guards were placed over him there.

Burke had been sought on the indictment issued yesterday.

Mr. and Mrs. G. H. Pfeuffer of Dallas, who registered at the tourist camp late today, heard a disturbance in an adjoining cabin and notified the proprietor, who investigated and found Burke lying wounded on the floor.

The indictment charges Burke misappropriated public funds in connection with the handling of a $7,500 city warrant of which he was trustee. It was brought out Wednesday in a court of inquiry conducted before Justice of the Peace J. R. Stappenbeck that the warrant, dated Feb. 6, 1930, had been placed in Burke's keeping pending the settlement of litigation which arose from condemnation by the city of certain property.

Burke first was taken tonight to the station hospital at Fort Sam Houston where Deputy Sheriffs Raymond Griffith and Lawrence Millard identified him by a gold watch found on his person.

Two misdemeanor complaints also were filed against him today by Grover C. Morris, assistant county attorney, in a county court at law, charging that Burke failed to seal up and deposit the warrant in a secure place, as required by law.

The moneyl involved was to pay for property belonging to P. A. Astoria, if an agreement could be reached between Astoria and the city. The litigation ended last week and a request for the money was made to Burke, but according to testimony at the inquiry before Justice Stappenbeck, he had failed to deliver it.

ROBBER FLEES UNDER GUNFIRE

Returning bullet for bullet, a young robber escaped in a hail of gunfire at 4:15 p. m. yesterday after taking $30 in cash and $400 in jewelry from the shop of Ben M. Brown, jeweler, 1302 Hemphill Street.

The robber fired the first shot as he left Brown's place of business after a woman customer had retreated against the intruder's orders and had spread the alarm.

Brown seized his own pistol and shot four times at the man as he fled south of Hemphill. The robber fired in return as he raced around the corner of a nearby building.

M. E. Simmons, 2100 Jennings Avenue, manager of an adjoining Piggly-Wiggly Store, took Brown's pistol and gave chase, leaping to the running board of a passing automob'le.

Simmons fired once into the air after calling out to the robber to halt as the man raced west on Myrtle Street. The man's answer was with bullets which flew wide of their mark.

Simmons then leveled his own pistol at the man, firing the remaining two shots. The man, Simmons related later, seemed to falter for a moment as if wounded, but he continued his flight and ducked among residences in the 1500 block of Alston Avenue.

The grocery manager stood guard until a police cordon was thrown around the area. A search of residences and outbuildings, however, was unavailing.

Brown said the robber, about 25, appeared extremely nervous as he ordered him to "stick 'em up." The jeweler was forced first to open his safe and permit the bandit to select gems and cash from its contents. He then ordered the jeweler to give him pieces of jewelry on display in the shop window. It was while the jeweler was complying that the woman customer entered with her son.

Soviet Points to Gains In First 5-Year Plan

(Copyright 1932, Associated Press.)

MOSCOW, Dec. 30.—Soviet Russia's five-year plan for economic construction, shortened to four years and three months, ends with the old year in undoubted industrial, agricultural and social achievements for the world's first socialistic state, but fulfilment only in part of the definite objectives it laid down.

From the viewpoint of Soviet leaders the plan has been successfully carried out in the attainment of its broad general aim of establishing a base for industrialization of the country.

The nation now has a foundation of heavy industry, they claim, on which can be built future means of production without relying on foreign imports.

the latest available figures of accomplishment, however, shows that the industrial plan as a whole has not been fulfilled. In some branches of economy it can be credited with successes far beyond the ambitious dreams of the planners themselves. In others, the country has fallen far short of the goals it set for itself.

Until complete and final figures are published, which may be several weeks it will be impossible to strike a balance of the actual successes and failures under the plan. A fair index for industry, however, can be found in the record of the greater part of this year, showing less than 20 per cent increase over 1931 in all industrial production, whereas a 34.7 increase

The Weather

Fort Worth—Saturday, generally fair.

West Texas—Generally fair Saturday; Sunday increasing cloudiness, slightly warmer in north portion.

East Texas—Fair, colder in east portion Saturday; Sunday fair, slightly warmer in north portion.

Oklahoma—Fair, slightly colder in east portion Saturday; Sunday partly coludy, rising temperature.

Arkansas—Generally fair and much colder Saturday; Sunday fair, rising temperature.

Louisiana—Partly cloudy and decidedly colder Saturday and Saturday night, probably freezing to the coast Saturday night; Sunday gen-

Sidelights Last Night at Salesmen's Roundup

Oscar Seligman, hero of Howard Peak's "Fifty Years a Ranger of Commerce," occupied a front row at a meeting of old, old drummers at the Salesmen's Roundup at The Texas last night.

"Times were sure different 50 years ago," he said. "Then all a salesman had to do was to let his customers know he was in town. He would sit around and gossip for a few hours, then go to bed. The next day his orders were delivered to him by his customers."

Incidentally, Seligman admits traveling in West Texas since 1873.

insurance is a far step, C. F. Webb says.

"Now, instead of teaching people to decline nouns, I must teach them to decline life insurance," he said. He was an instructor in the Fort Worth schools for many years.

Henry Keller, city secretary-treasurer, just managed to prove his eligibility to be called a salesman. He was stopped at the door by A. J. Wylie, general chairman.

"What is your business?" Wylie asked.

"I am a salesman," Keller replied.

Hoover and Party Land 10 Sailfish During Day

By Associated Press.

SAIL FISH CLUB, PALM BEACH, Fla., Dec. 30. — Running into a veritable school of fighting sail fish late today, President Hoover and members of his party tonight brought in 10 prizes as the total of a dawn-to-dusk angling expedition in the wind-whipped waters of the Atlantic Ocean off Palm Beach.

The Chief Executive himself landed three of the sail fish, one seven feet and eight inches long. The total for the party would have been 11 except that a shark, whirling to the surface in a smother of foam, snatched a prize from Senator Austin of Vermont just before it was hurled into the boat.

after daybreak, the Hoover party had only mediocre luck during much of the day. Until midafternoon only three of the white flags that signify a sail fish catch were visible from the balyards of the two boats.

During the late afternoon, however, one fish after another was landed. In addition to the three caught by Hoover, Dr. Joel T. Boone, the White House physician, also landed three; Justice Stone of the Supreme Court, two; Lawrence Richey, White House secretary, one, and Mark Sullivan, writer, one.

After returning to the Sequoia, anchored in Lake Worth here, shortly after 6 o'clock tonight, the President was made an honorary member of the

On the 3rd Saturday of February, 1846, a group of settlers met at the log cabin of Charles Throop and formed Lonesome Dove Baptist Church, led by Reverend David Myers and Reverend John Freeman. At the time of the church's founding, there were no other churches within many miles and no other evangelical church between Lonesome Dove and the Pacific Ocean.

In 1886, Charles Throop sold the cabin to the Torian family, who resided in the cabin until the 1940s. The Torian family is pictured above.

In 1976, the Grapevine Historical Society was given a 48-hour notice to save the cabin from being demolished. Society members numbered each log with nail polish as it was torn down to ensure accurate reconstruction. The cabin was moved four miles, from Dove Road to Main Street, and now sits at Liberty Park. Spectators can peek through glass panels and view the furnishings to get an idea of what life was like in the 1800s.

The Torian Cabin is the oldest standing building in Tarrant County.

Lonesome Dove Baptist Church June 1894

Lonesome Dove Baptist Church, which still stands today in Southlake, Texas, was named when a dove landed on Reverend David Myers' shoulder one day while preaching in a nearby arbor. This was taken as a sign and a church was built on the very same spot.

Many years later, author Larry McMurtry, while dining at a restaurant in Oklahoma, saw a Lonesome Dove Baptist Church van and thought the name would be a good one for the town in a novel he was writing. *Lonesome Dove* won a Pulitzer Prize in 1986 and in 1989 became a TV series.

The family tree flourished in Grapevine. Reverend David Myers' great, great, great granddaughter, Debi (Metker) Meek owns Bermuda Gold & Silver on Main Street and is the caretaker of the Torian Cabin.

In 1859, Thomas Jefferson Nash purchased a 110-acre spot of land and log cabin with his wife, Elizabeth Nash, and it bears their name today, Nash Farm. Ten years after his purchase, Thomas built a farmhouse (which still stands today) for his family of nine. Around 1900, Mrs. Nash was one of the first Grapevine residents to have a telephone. Her phone number was 7 and her telephone signal was two rings. In those days, each home had its own phone signal. This was the beginning of caller I.D. and the notion of "not hearing the phone ring" when that annoying relative calls during dinnertime.

Turn off the cell phones, unplug the video games, and transport back in time to 19th-century farm life. Each year Nash Farm, the oldest operating farmstead in Tarrant County, hosts an interesting array of seasonal events, interpretive programs, and exhibits to educate visitors about our heritage. Participants experience a simpler, yet much more difficult, lifestyle and challenges faced by settlers in the formative years of our society. Authentic period attire completes the Nash Farm experience.

Kitchen gardening, cotton picking, cow milking, and washboard laundering are just a few of the chores you may never be able to convince your kids to do outside of Nash Farm. These hands-on demonstrations will convince your youngsters that life is good in the 21st century!

It's difficult to imagine the good ol' days, and I imagine the good ol' days were difficult. We can read about the old days, hear great-grandma's stories, or watch *Bonanza* reruns, but to experience it makes it real. Explore bygone days at Nash Farm.

Children under the age of six often bedded in the master bedroom and slept on an early version of a trundle bed. The bottom frame of the trundle was laced with ropes to provide support, and the ropes would be tightened before bed.

According to popular belief, the expression "sleep tight" originated from this practice.

A vintage 1892 wood-burning stove is used for cooking demonstrations in the Nash Farm kitchen.

How do you preheat this oven to 375 degrees to cook a frozen lasagna?

The barn, located near the farmhouse, is home to Gulf Coast sheep.

This breed of sheep was brought to America by New World settlers beginning in the 1500s.

These Spanish descendants do not have wool on their faces, legs, or bellies as a result of their successful adaptation to heat and humidity in the South.

Established in the late 1800s, Austin Ranch is one of the oldest dude ranches in Texas. Today, the ranch is a premier destination for corporate events, fund-raisers, family reunions, and team building events.

The party facility was founded in 1956 by Dr. Frank and Ruby Austin. Dr. Austin is a descendant of famed Texas hero Stephen F. Austin, and the ranch carries his brand as a logo.

The unique menu of team building events and attractions at Austin Ranch are sure to keep party aficionados entertained. A few crowd favorites include broken-glass walking, firewalking, stick horse barrel racing, corn shucking, rubber chicken plucking, and armadillo racing.

Men gathered at Shelton's Barber Shop in 1931 for the occasional 25-cent haircut, 15-cent shave, and to catch up on the latest news.

"Sometimes as a kid, I hung out at Mr. Jackson's and Mr. Stewart's barber shops. It was a chance to catch up on the gossip. I learned a lot there after the war - stuff I probably shouldn't have known."

-Mayor William D. Tate

Today, Main Street Barber Shop offers an ultimate old-time experience. Patrons step back in time as they relax in old-fashioned barber chairs while snacking on free popcorn during their trim. Vintage pieces adorning the shop include a mechanical coin horse, old-fashioned soda machines, antique ice cream coolers, and of course, the traditional barber pole both inside and on the street.

If you're feeling adventurous, the menu includes straight-razor face shaves.

In the early 1900s, cantaloupes were planted where Delaney Vineyards resides today.

In 1935, cantaloupes were "King" and Grapevine crowned a Cantaloupe Queen. The Grapevine Lions Club sponsored the town's first Cantaloupe Festival and at least 100 truckloads of melons were delivered, enjoyed, and purchased by attendees. Competition and contests were highlights of the festival. Clarence F. Millican, a Main Street café owner, took first place in the cantaloupe eating contest that first year, by consuming 26 melons. The last Cantaloupe Festival coincided with the start of WWII in 1941.

Grapevine was known as the Cantaloupe Center of the USA.

The spirit of festival competition has remained alive over the decades. GrapeFest® wine festival, established in 1987, offers attendees the chance to hop into a wine barrel and participate in the age-old tradition of grape stomping.

Teams of two are given two minutes to stomp as much juice as possible out of 18 pounds of grapes.

Feet have been used to crush grapes for thousands of years. It is believed the method of grape stomping was used to produce wine drank by the ancient Romans in 200 B.C.

After everyone's favorite redhead, Lucille Ball, famously stomped grapes in a 1950s *I Love Lucy* episode, grape stomping contests sprang up all over the country. Thankfully, no feet are used to generate any of the wine distributed at GrapeFest.

Selling wine produced from grape treading has been outlawed in the U.S. for about a century.

In the early 1900s, the Grapevine Cornet and Concert Bands entertained residents and visitors. The 1920s and 1930s brought the popularity of fiddle bands. The Rabbit Twisters was one of the best known in the Grapevine area with regular live shows on WFAA Radio. Popular fiddle bands played at the Cantaloupe Festival, in parades, and at special events.

The Grapevine Jam

The more things change, the more they remain the same. Although the music scene has changed quite drastically, residents and visitors still gather to enjoy the sounds of local musicians in multiple venues throughout Grapevine.

The Grapevine Jam, a local favorite established in 2009, draws crowds to evenings of classic rock, country, and old-time favorites. Numerous familiar faces fill the crowd as old friends come together and all the "regulars" know everybody's name. The band has evolved from a small jam session to filling Farina's Winery & Cafe to standing-room only status, thanks to the contributions of Sharron Spencer, the "World's Best Road Manager."

The Walton Stout Band

Grapevine's annual street festivals also bring out bands of all varieties to entertain even the most eclectic music lover. Young and old, there's no shortage of fans showing off their best moves in front of the crowds. Modern day technology and pyrotechnics have advanced the visual experience, but the good old-fashioned feeling is still very much intact.

The two-story Wallis Hotel, also referred to as the Brick Hotel, was built in 1891 by John Wallis for his sister, Susan. The hotel accommodated traveling salesmen and agricultural business leaders arriving by train. Although Grapevine has always been known as a safe town, the hotel had a separate entrance for ladies to shield them from the "rougher" aspects of 19th-century society.

The hotel was never a financial success and closed its doors in 1926. It was demolished in the mid 1930s.

100 years after the Wallis hotel was built, in 1991, a replica of the hotel was built a few blocks north of the original site. The replica was built to office the Grapevine Convention & Visitors Bureau (CVB). The CVB occupied the building until 2012 when the offices were moved directly across the street from the original Wallis Hotel location. In 2014, Messina Hof Winery moved into the Wallis Hotel replica.

A small museum, located on the 2nd floor of Messina Hof Winery, displays photos and artifacts of the original hotel once located down the street.

Farmers proudly displayed their new farm equipment as they made their way down Main Street for all to view in the 1899 Binder Parade.

A century later, a twinkle in Santa's eye and a magnificent light show illuminate Main Street. The Parade of Lights is known as the largest lighted Christmas parade in North Texas, celebrating the season with more than 100 illuminated floats, marching bands, classic cars, and a grand appearance by St. Nick.

Built in 1940, the Grapevine Ice Company produced 10 tons of ice per day. The company delivered ice blocks to Grapevine and surrounding towns. Each home had an "ice card" to place in a window to indicate the size of the ice block they desired. The ice block was stored in the family ice box to keep perishables cold. The plant's operations were halted in the early 1970s and the building was demolished in 1974.

The Grapevine Historical Society was established in 1972 to save the Cotton Belt Railroad Depot from being demolished. In 1974, the society established the historical museum and its home was inside the train depot for 40 years. In 2014, the museum moved into a renovated 1970s building with an exterior facade that replicates the 1940 Grapevine Ice Company.

The Grapevine Historical Museum features unique items originating in Grapevine. Some of the treasures include a human hair wreath, a wooden washing machine, and cast footprints from a Hadrosaur dinosaur. The dinosaur's footprints were uncovered during a 1981 flood of Grapevine Lake. Additional dinosaur footprints and remains have been discovered throughout the area after floods and droughts.

In olden times, premature burial stories were not uncommon. Families would sit beside the body of a loved one for hours or even days in case the person should awaken; hence, today's practice of holding a "wake" prior to burial services.

The funeral industry evolved after the Civil War. Embalming became more accepted after Abraham Lincoln's body was embalmed before being transported by train from Washington D.C. to Springfield, IL for burial. Paying respects to the dead and their family in a funeral parlor instead of the family home, as was commonly practiced, also became prevalent. Additionally, as in the case with the Lucas family, undertakers and their families often lived in the funeral homes, and family members assisted in business matters.

The exterior wooden sign at this renovated circa 1900 dwelling once read, "J.T. Lucas Funeral Home" and now reads, "Esparza's Restaurante Mexicano."

Locally known as The Margarita Capital of Texas, Esparza's is also known for its impressive outdoor patio scene; the perfect place to enjoy that frozen or "on the rocks" beverage.

In 1890, J.E. Foust & Co. general store sold dry goods and funeral supplies allowing shoppers to pick up sugar and a coffin in a one-stop shop. In the late 1800s, it was common for coffins and funeral supplies to be sold in dry good stores and other retail outlets.

Owner John E. Foust, Sr. was also responsible for installing Grapevine's first rural telephone around 1900, and by 1909 he had furnished telephone service to the entire community.

In 1945, the Foust family opened J.E. Foust & Son Funeral Home, where the family also resided. They were the last family to live on South Main Street, until 2007, when luxury apartments were built at Main Street and Dallas Road.

In 1980, the funeral home, which still stands today, buried a time capsule to be opened in 2080.

Good Things for All Seasons now sits in the former J.E. Foust & Co. general store building and is the oldest brick building on Main Street. To say this place has all of your seasonal decorating needs covered would be an understatement. The elaborate exterior décor that changes each season, coupled with everything from mazes of marvelous miniature Halloween towns to star spangled accessories and colorful Christmas ornaments covering every wall, makes it a site worth seeing.

Goin' places that I've never been,

Seein' things that I may never see again,

And I can't wait to get on the road again.

—Willie Nelson

Steam Engine No. 2248, affectionately known as "Puffy," was built on August 29, 1896 at Cook Locomotive Works in Patterson, New Jersey. The engine was used by Southern Pacific Railroad for many years.

Puffy retired in 1959 when her flue time* expired. She was purchased by a private collector who had plans with Walt Disney to build a steam railroad system around Griffith Park in Los Angeles. Luckily for Grapevine, their plans did not materialize. On the locomotive's 100th birthday, August 29, 1996, Puffy arrived in Grapevine.

The turntable used to rotate Puffy was purchased and had to be transported from Saginaw to Grapevine within 48 hours. The unbelievable price tag for the piece was only $1, but the expedited move cost $10,000! Shipping and handling charges are always the catch.

Today, the Grapevine Vintage Railroad is serviced by two locomotives; Puffy, the oldest continuously operating steam engine in the South and oldest operating engine still using its original boiler, and "Vinny," a 1953 GP-7 diesel locomotive. The engines pull four luxurious Victorian 1925 day coaches and two 1927 open-air touring coaches.

*Flue time - The flue (a common name for a boiler fire tube - the pipes that circulate the water) has a set amount of run time before requiring a rebuild. Instead of doing a rebuild, which was very costly and labor intensive, once the flue time expired, most companies scrapped the engines. As a result, more efficient engines were developed resulting in the extinction of steam engines. Most steam engines were out of service by the late 1940s or very early 1950s.

The Grapevine Vintage Railroad makes regular trips carrying visitors from Historic Downtown Grapevine to the Fort Worth Stockyards. The train pulls into an indoor station where visitors of the popular whistle stop gather round to welcome the massive incoming entourage.

The area is filled with historic venues that are within walking distance of the train station.

Billy Bob's Texas, the world's largest honky tonk, is located in a circa 1910 building that was once an open-air barn used for housing prize cattle during the Fort Worth Stock Show. The establishment now has a concert stage that has welcomed many world-renowned artists, several dance floors, a restaurant, video arcade, and, as a tribute to its heritage - a small live bull-riding arena. Johnny Cash, Garth Brooks, Waylon Jennings, and many other celebrities have left their mark at Billy Bob's Texas. A wall of casted celebrity handprints graces the entrance.

The Stockyards Championship Rodeo, the world's only year-round rodeo, is held every weekend in the Cowtown Coliseum. The Coliseum was built in 1908, in just 88 working days, and is home to the world's first indoor rodeo. The "King of Rock and Roll," Elvis Presley, performed at the Coliseum a number of times in the 1950s.

Fort Worth is also famous for the world's only twice-daily cattle drive of The Fort Worth Herd. On June 12th of 1999, as 15,000 spectators looked on, The Fort Worth Herd made its first cattle drive through the Fort Worth Stockyards National Historic District.

Bonnie and Clyde, who frequented Grapevine, are also intertwined in Fort Worth's intriguing history. The couple stayed at The Stockyards Hotel in the midst of their crime spree and left one night in such a hurry that Bonnie left her gun behind. The gun remains on display, to this day, in the Bonnie and Clyde suite.

Grapevine Lake opened in 1952. To commemorate the occasion, future Grapevine Mayor, William D. Tate, a young boy at the time, released the first fish into their new home.

The Federal Government aquired 15,700 acres for the lake. At conservation level, the lake covers 7,280 acres. The man-made lake includes 60 miles of shoreline and attracts over one million visitors each year.

The U.S. Army Corps of Engineers, who built the lake, predicted it would take over five years to fill. The rains came and filled the lake much quicker. Some construction machinery and equipment was not moved due to the quick fill and still remains at the bottom of the lake.

Voted in 2014 by US Today as one of the top ten best urban campgrounds, The Vineyards Campground & Cabins on Grapevine Lake has 93 campsites, 15 climate-controlled waterfront cabins, and a private boat ramp accessible to registered campers and their guests.

"In June and July, the crops matured and grasshoppers came to town like a plague. I would collect them in a paper sack hoping dad would take me fishing."

-Mayor William D. Tate

Dallas/Fort Worth (DFW) International Airport opened in 1974 and the first commercial flight was American Airlines flight 241. Forty years later in 2014, based on the number of flights, it was identified by Airports Council International as the third busiest airport in the world. The average number of daily passengers is more than 170,000 and each of these travelers can reach any major U.S. city within four hours.

The colossal waypoint covers 26.9 square miles and 17,207 acres, making it larger than the island of Manhattan, NY. With a whopping 42,000 parking spots, remembering where you parked your car may be an added vacation adventure.

Grapevine's first volunteer fire department was organized in 1908 and was comprised of 13 volunteers. They were affectionately known as the "Bucket Brigade." In 1915, the city authorized a payment of $2 to the Fire Chief for every fire he and his volunteer team attended. The first motorized fire truck was purchased in 1917 for $300 and was equipped with soda and acid tanks. In 1965, a salary of $325 per month was approved for the city's first paid firemen.

Things have come a long way. The Grapevine Fire Department now employs more than 100 firefighters and deploys over two dozen vehicles including engines, trucks, and boats from five separate stations.

Introducing the vivacious and curvy Miss Grapevine...truck. The 1931 half-ton Chevrolet pickup truck operated as a portable grape crusher for many years in the vineyards of Sonoma Valley, California. The truck facilitated efficient on-site grape pressing and movement of grapes from vineyard to vineyard. In 2005, Miss Grapevine made the journey from California to Texas. She often makes an appearance at Grapevine festivals, events, and parades.

You are now entering the Urban Wine Trail, which, like a hearty vineyard, is always expanding. Thanks to Franciscan priests, North America's first vineyard sprouted circa 1662, and its home was in Texas. The Lone Star State is now one of the nation's largest wine producers.

Grapevine is home to the Texas wine industry headquarters and it's no coincidence; the city has a long history of wineries - some haunted, some historic, and some in unique locations. One of the first winery tasting rooms in Grapevine was located in a former Church of Christ.

Wine connoisseurs around the globe have Texas legend T.V. Munson to thank for saving the wine industry. In the late 1860s, European vineyards were plagued with Phylloxera, a microscopic root-eating insect related to the aphid. More than 6 million acres of vineyards were destroyed in France, Germany, and other European regions.

Munson discovered that grafting a hearty Texas grape vine stock to other vines would strengthen them. He identified a rootstock that would best adapt to soil conditions in Europe and supplied the French with cuttings to revive their vineyards.

"You're welcome."
         -Texas

 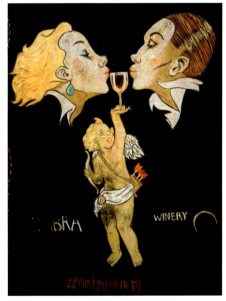 

um·bra
noun

1. The darkest part of a shadow cast by Earth, the Moon, or another body during an eclipse.

300 pounds of selenite stone, a white, crystalline, transparent-to-translucent gypsum, fills Umbra Winery's wet bar, and are custom colored to resemble a contrast to the "Umbra."

The winery also features unique, one-of-a-kind wine vials created by chemical engineer, owner, and wine maker John Wilson. The vials are equipped with air pumps, allowing visitors the full olfactory experience of their wines. The brick and stone showing through the interior walls are the original early 1900s building materials. If these walls could talk, they'd probably have forgotten what they wanted to say.

Golden statues from the original 1891 Wallis Hotel, atop the staircase posts, welcome visitors entering Messina Hof Winery. The 1800s motif of an old western saloon and hotel takes patrons back to a simpler time. Wooden nickels, like the ones used briefly in the 19th century, are used as wine tasting tokens.

Founded in 1977, with the original location in Bryan, Texas, Messina Hof opened its Grapevine location in the replicated Wallis Hotel in 2014. An estimated 60,000 cases of wine are produced each year to serve Messina Hof's three wineries. The Historic Downtown Grapevine urban winery features a wine dispensing system showcasing nine wines on tap. The nine offerings change weekly.

Grape Vine Springs Winery has had upwards of 5,000 bottles of wine on the wall. Take one down, pass it around, and you've got the longest song ever. Limited edition bottles feature labels with a dose of rich and full-bodied sarcasm. The interactive establishment allows patrons to create their own wine labels and partake in wine tastings which are served over 16,000 times annually.

Interested in a good scare? Grapevine's Night Watchman Ghost Tour, hosted by Grape Vine Springs Winery, is a spine-tingling walking journey through Historic Downtown Grapevine. The stories and legends of Grapevine's paranormal experiences will have you sleeping with one eye open.

Surrounded by centuries-old Oak and Pecan trees, Cross Timbers Winery is located in what is believed to be the fifth oldest structure in Grapevine. Their signature wines complement the unique indoor and outdoor venue that's perfect for weddings, parties, catching up with friends, or a romantic date.

Located in an 1895 Folk Victorian style home, Homestead Winery dons the original wood floors and fireplace. The owners saw the writing on the wall and decided to add more. Patrons are encouraged to leave their John Hancock or short sentiment where they see fit. In 2010, a wedding proposal was penned on the wall. The wine is that good!

Roughly 9,000 vines wind through Delaney Vineyards. The 10-acre farm is the only fully operational and working vineyard and winery in the North Texas region. Each row of vines is capped with planted "lucky roses" called as such because bugs will attack the rose bushes first. The attraction to the flowering buds is an early alert system; the preemptive spraying of the vines saves the grapes.

Operations are run from a beautiful building modeled after an 18th-century French chateau. The building houses the tank room with tanks capable of holding 3,000 gallons of wine, translating to 1,260 cases of wine per tank. That would make for one heck of a party, which Delaney often hosts in the form of corporate events, weddings, and other private parties.

The Oak wine barrels, used to age the wine, and displayed in the tasting room, aren't held together with glue or nails. They are sealed by swelling the wood until nothing can leak through. Each barrel is used for about four cycles before being retired. An Italian-made bottling machine is another stop in the process before wine reaches the shelves. The machine is capable of bottling 1,500 bottles per hour.

The ceiling of a beautiful foyer just inside the main entrance displays a magnificent painting that tells the age-old story of when monks were the primary wine makers. The story goes that when the monks arrived to the caves to test the wooden tonnes of their wine, they often found their barrels to be missing a bit of wine; they didn't understand that wine evaporates through the wood. With theft being the logical rationale for the absent wine, bigger and heavier doors were built, with locks added to the cave entrance. Wine still went missing. Through prayer, the monks determined that angels must be guarding the vineyard and their wine, and as compensation for their service, a little wine, of course. The angels in the foyer painting, "Circle of Angels," are enjoying the fruits of their labor.

Nine percent of U.S. businesses are owned by veterans, one of which is located in the heart of Historic Downtown Grapevine. U.S. Army Veterans, Alan W. Kunst, Jr. (the winemaker) and Ralph S. Mattison, Jr. (the wine drinker) are the founders, proprietors, and wine producers of Sloan & Williams Winery.

The sweetest surprise when visiting Sloan & Williams is the wine ice cream - that's right - wine ice cream. In partnership with Mercer's Dairy out of New York, the winery carries a plethora of wine-infused ice creams and is the only spot in Grapevine it can be found. You can have your cake and eat it too, but rarely can you have your wine and eat it too. Only here can you have wine with dinner, with dessert, and for dessert. How sweet it is. God bless America.

Sloan & Williams Winery is located in a 100-year-old building owned by the Grapevine Masonic Lodge. The Masonic Lodge has occupied the building since 1916.

Grapevine Masonic Lodge was founded in 1866 with a humble 14 members and is now nearly 200 strong. When the Masonic Lodge first formed, the meetings were held in a storage shed about one mile north of what is now downtown Grapevine.

Eight of Grapevine's 18 mayors, at some point, belonged to Grapevine Masonic Lodge.

Farina's Winery & Cafe serves over 100 wines from around the world, along with a few of their own blends. The wine complements Farina's original family recipes, one of which is the Muffaletta sandwich.

The Muffaletta recipe is in honor of owner Gary Farina's grandfather who made a solo trip from Sicily to America at age nine. When he arrived in New Orleans, he made contact with his family at Central Grocery, where the first Muffaletta sandwich was invented.

The wet bar located on Farina's back patio traveled across the great pond from the Manchester United boardroom. Manchester United is the world's first professional sports team to be valued at more than $3 billion, according to *Forbes Magazine*. The professional football club (soccer in the U.S.) is based in Old Trafford, Greater Manchester, England.

The crown jewel of Farina's is hanging in the main dining room. The grape chandelier, created by Blenko Glass (established in 1893) was commissioned by the City of Grapevine and auctioned at the 2004 GrapeFest®. The makers literally broke the mold after creating this astounding one-of-a-kind piece.

Photograph by Mark Pavlovich

Su Vino Winery®, established in 2003, translates from Italian and Spanish to "Your Wine," and that is precisely what they deliver. Not only can patrons use their creative genius in designing their own label, but the wine also can be uniquely crafted to please and excite each, one-of-a-kind palate. Wine lovers can complete the process with the hands-on experience of bottling and corking their own wine. Enjoy!

"Dugout," a featured Bingham Family Vineyards wine, was named after the Bingham's ancestors who homesteaded in dugouts in the early 1900s upon settling in Texas.

Bingham Family Vineyards produces approximately 1.5 million ounces of wine each year to stock their Grapevine tasting room and other locations throughout Texas. The Bingham's have farmed grapes, peanuts, and organic cotton at their 200-acre farm in Lubbock, Texas for over five generations.

The logo design reflects this musically talented family of eleven children.

Captivatingly clad in industrial modern décor, Wine Fusion Winery quickly made a name for itself. It is known to be the only winery in Texas to offer patrons an opportunity to craft a single bottle of their very own unique red or white blend wines.

Deeper dives into the art form can be achieved by participating in wine and food pairing classes. The option to simply have a glass of wine or two, or six, is always on the table as well.

Grapevine hosts a number of festivals and events throughout the year drawing crowds from neighboring cities, states, and countries around the world. In 2012, Grapevine received the distinguished honor of being named a World Festival & Event City by the International Festivals & Events Association. Grapevine's two flagship street festivals are Main Street Fest and GrapeFest®.

GrapeFest is the largest wine festival in the Southwest, with annual attendance averaging over 260,000 during the four-day event. One of the most popular attractions at GrapeFest is the People's Choice Wine Tasting Classic, the largest consumer-judged wine competition in the United States, featuring more than 160 wines from over 40 wineries.

Are you supposed to cork an open bottle of champagne if you don't finish the bottle? Well, the French advise you to drink it; that's just one less thing to have to worry about.

No time to count the tiny bubbles in a bottle of champagne here. A GrapeFest® crowd favorite is the Champagne Cork Shoot-Off. Hundreds gather to cheer on participants as they shake their champagne and shoot their cork to the best of their ability. Markers identify festival and world records, and just like the measurements on a golf driving range, they are only there to taunt you.

All aboard! Jazz Wine Train passengers are treated to multiple wine tastings from featured Grapevine winery tasting rooms. Like a proper wine tasting, Jazz Wine Train has the perfect accompaniment to complete the experience. Along with the hors d'oeuvres and desserts, this annual trip to yesteryear is graced with jazz musicians serenading and entertaining passengers as they rotate throughout the moving train cars. The event is punctuated with a grand finale show on the train depot platform.

Jesus' first miracle was turning water into wine. Thank you, Jesus.

An annual Grapevine tradition for more than 20 years, "Blessing of the Vines" originated in Europe during the emergence of Christianity. In 1598, the tradition crossed the pond and entered the New World, to the area known today as El Paso, Texas.

Spanish missionaries planted vineyards for ceremonial wines and blessed the vines to ensure robust vines and savory grapes each year.

Virtually unchanged over the last 400 years, the blessing, performed by a priest, asks for God's grace upon the vines, the fruit they produce, and for the safety and health of those tending the vines.

The ceremony commences with a procession through the beautiful Delaney Vineyards led by a mariachi band, the Knights of Columbus, and a carried statue of Saint Urban, the patron saint of vineyards. Look-a-likes of Bacchus (also known as Dionysus), the Roman God of wine, and Ariadne, his immortal wife, often grace the event.

Those in attendance receive wine samples during the event, so ultimately, everyone is blessed.

The festivities continue on the New Vintage Wine and Gallery Trail. Wine glasses runneth over with blessings of new vintage wine releases, live music and beautiful works of art displayed at the many galleries throughout Historic Downtown Grapevine. Event "passports" can be purchased and presented in exchange for food and wine tastings at each winery tasting room. Explore the wine trail by foot, or for those not wearing boots made for walking, free shuttles are available to carry visitors to each location.

Father Ken Robinson

Take a seat next to *The Sidewalk Judge*, a sculpture created by J. Seward Johnson Jr. in 1997 to commemorate old-timers who sat similarly and judged or "people watched" passing strangers who visited Grapevine. People from around the world have sat for a picture and shared their secrets with the judge, a perpetual good listener.

The Sidewalk Judge is one of more than 25 pieces of art found along the Grapevine Public Art Trail. The trail features life-size sculptures, wall murals, art galleries, and working art studios.

Grapevine is known to be one of the only locations in the world with four neighboring "hot art" working studios, meaning that heat, and in most cases fire, is used as part of the artists' medium.

It's no secret that art and wine are a great pairing; you will likely find both around every corner.

The Grapevine Convention & Visitors Bureau (CVB), established in 1974, markets Grapevine and promotes local events and venues. With 11 million city visitors year, it's no wonder the headquarters of the Grapevine CVB is an attraction in and of itself.

Opened in 2012, the CVB complex is comprised of six facades, each commemorating an era in Grapevine's agriculture and commercial heritage. The most prominent facade is the Cotton Belt Hotel. The 127-foot-tall, brick hotel tower is topped with a 25-foot-tall "evergreen tree" tile roof, a tradition that migrated to America many years ago with European craftsmen. An evergreen was placed on the highest point of a building to symbolize growth and good luck.

High above the entrance, the brick tower is adorned with a 19th-century style vertical clock, temperature gauge, and weather vane. The building stands in honor of the men and women who settled in Grapevine during the 19th century.

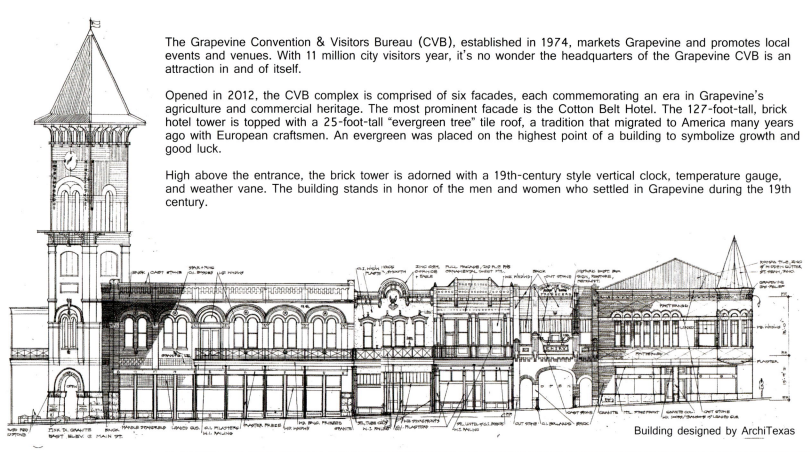

Building designed by ArchiTexas

Venetian style architecture and Palladian-design marble floors are a welcoming spectacle to those entering the Grapevine Visitor Information Center, located on the first floor of the Grapevine Convention & Visitors Bureau (CVB).

More than 100 years ago, grand staircases were the focal point of a building's entry and were commonly found in courthouses and public facilities. The CVB entry features a grand staircase, the treads of which were built in three phases to secure their width and grandeur. Located on each side of the staircase are the Grand and Tower Galleries. Exhibits rotate frequently and range from science and history to abstract art and sculptures.

Grapevine is home to one of the last things someone would expect to see in America, a giant glockenspiel. There aren't any cuckoo birds or Lederhosen clad figurines coming out of this clock; this is Texas, after all. Instead, two 9-foot-tall, gun-slinging, robotic cowboys participate in a shootout after they discover they're both in town to rob the same train.

Robo-bandits Nat and Willy saunter out of a 127-foot-high tower, six-shooters in hand, each ready to claim the approaching train as his own. The two *Would-Be Train Robbers* come to realize that, distracted by their boisterous dispute, they have both missed the train. A short mosey back into their respective saloon style doors and all is peaceful until the big and little hands call them back out again. For all the old-time gamblers watching, the winner of each duel is electronically selected at random.

The moral of the story - train robbin' doesn't pay.

Standing over 6 feet tall with a wingspan of 9 feet, *Imagine* is a tribute to all who work and volunteer in Grapevine's tourism and hospitality industry and symbolizes action, dreams, and wishes that come true.

The 800-pound bronze statue, created by Linda Lewis-Roarke, sits atop the Grapevine Convention & Visitors Bureau's north tower, flying 50 feet above the sidewalk. The colorful base of fused glass represents the growth and prosperity created by the crops of Grapevine throughout the years.

Before the Grapevine Police Department protected its citizens, the nightwatchman kept order, ensured businesses were locked at night, and even served as a dog catcher.

The Grapevine Nightwatchman bronze monument, created by Jack Bryant, sits atop City Hall immortalizing the men who served the post. The statue holds a glowing lantern and stands 8 feet tall, weighing 640 pounds.

If this is representative of an actual nightwatchman's size, it's no surprise Grapevine has always been such a safe town.

A replica statue was given to sister cities, Krems, Austria and Parras de la Fuente, Mexico.

Grapevine's first Nightwatchman, William Madison Bennett, 1907

Grapevine law enforcement dates back to 1907, and in 1911 a salary of $25 per month was authorized for the town marshal.

The first patrol car was purchased in 1953 for use by the marshal and nightwatchman. That same year, the marshal was authorized to begin issuing traffic tickets to violators, which is only logical because it would've been difficult to catch and fine a speeding motorist on a horse with only one horsepower.

Today, the Grapevine Police Department employs nearly 100 officers. More than 40 vehicles including squad cars, motorcycles, mobile command units, and all-terrain vehicles are used to keep the city safe.

Grapevine nightwatchman clock displayed inside City Hall

The life-sized *Sunday Skaters* depict three young children who grew up in Grapevine during the 1920s and 1930s. The statues were created by Archie St. Clair from photographs of the children: Mary Virginia, J.E., and Dorothy Bess.

The skaters, chaperoned by their dog, remind visitors of a simpler time in Grapevine. The dog, Muttin, represents a real character that belonged to one of Grapevine's dedicated nightwatchmen, James "Uncle Jim" Daniel. The piece was dedicated in 2006.

Norman Rockwell would be proud.

Nightwatchman, James Daniel and his dog, Muttin in 1929.

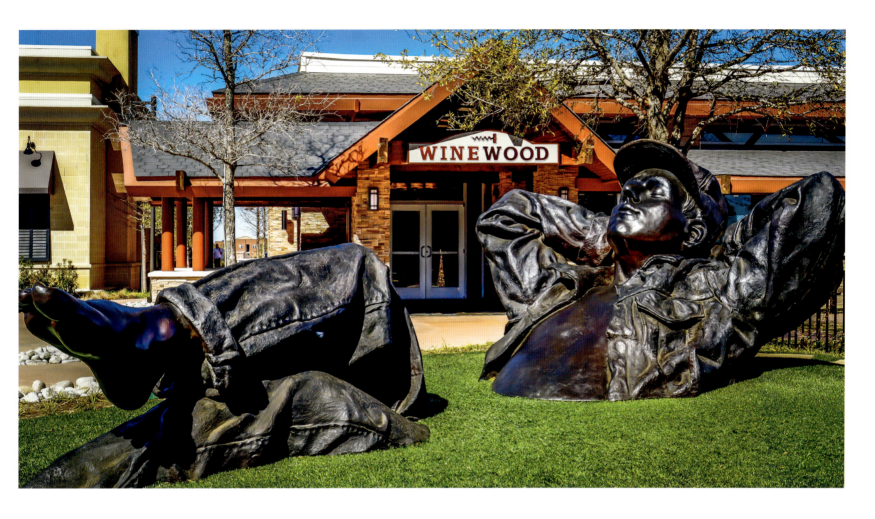

The triple life-size bronze sculpture *Pastoral Dreamer* is one of seven identical pieces with replicas located throughout the United States including Chicago and Minneapolis. The original piece was commissioned by the University of Oklahoma. Californian creator, David L. Phelps, envisioned the creation in a moment of extreme fatigue after spending countless hours in his studio. He turned his body during a long stretch and caught a glimpse of a wax head sculpture leaning in a corner against a wall. This vision became the reality of a 5-foot-tall, 17-foot-long day dreaming boy.

David remembers a constant worry about drought as a child. When the rains finally came, everyone worried about high water. His art, often emerging from the ground, is the embodiment of these constant opposing forces of the environment.

Benjamin Richard "B.R." Wall was Grapevine's fourth mayor and served the city for over 20 years making him the second-longest-serving mayor in the city's history. B.R. Wall was known for his optimism, charisma, and progressive ideas. Standing as tribute to his service, this life-size bronze statue features a wire loop in which a passerby can place a fresh rose - something B.R. Wall was known for wearing during his tenure as mayor. This statue, created by Archie St. Clair, was dedicated in 2004.

Catch a glimpse of Grapevine history. In 1986, artist Deborah Vest painted a historical collage on Western Auto's north wall to celebrate the Texas sesquicentennial. Facing the gazebo, the mural depicts a parade day in Grapevine, featuring the Grapevine Concert Band, J.E. Foust & Co. general store, and memories of days past.

Beloved painter, extraordinary entertainer, opera singer, and impersonator Jorge D'Soria was commissioned by the Grapevine Masonic Lodge to paint the 16 most legendary Masons in this 33' x 10' wall mural. The piece was completed in 2009. Jorge started painting at age five and includes a disguised self-profile in most of his paintings.

With more than 15 years of experience as a sculptor, Linda Lewis-Roark is the proud owner of the Grapevine Foundry and Fine Arts Program.

For those unfamiliar with the practice, a foundry is an establishment where metals are superheated, melted, and poured into hand-crafted molds. When the metal hardens and the molds are removed, a sculpture is born.

Viewing areas surrounding the foundry give spectators a glimpse at the process. Classes are also offered for those wanting a deeper dive into metal sculpting. Linda makes it look easy, but from the flame resistant suit to the near 1,800 degree molten metal, this is one truly hot and tough job.

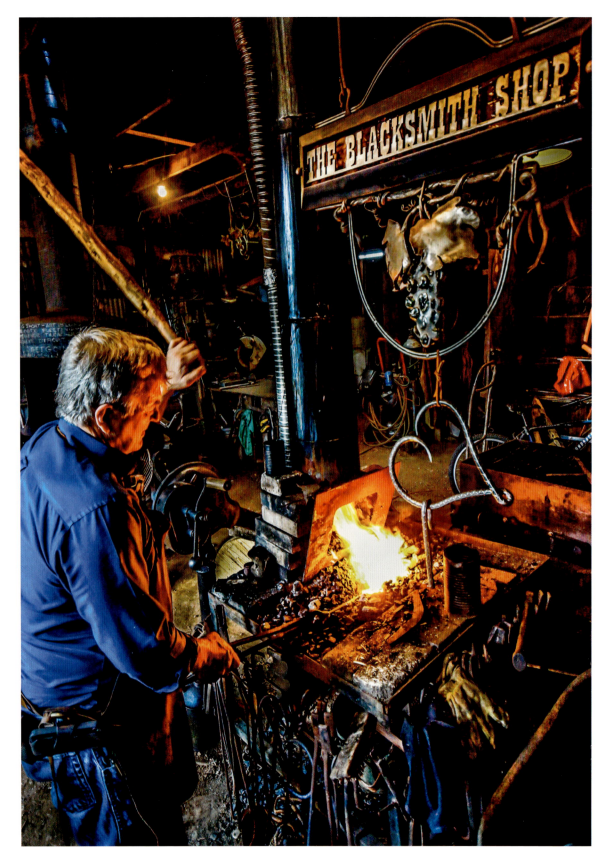

The first reference of the art of blacksmithing dates back to sometime around 3,000 B.C.

In 1909, Charles Millican had a blacksmith shop in Grapevine where he worked for more than 50 years. In 1995, a replica of the shop was built in the Heritage Center. In olden days, blacksmiths tested the precision of their branding irons by burning a symbol into the door of the shop. Similar iron burns can be found on the doors of the replicated blacksmith shop.

Today, Will Frary keeps the tradition alive with hand-forged works of art made from recycled iron, railroad spikes, rebar, and horseshoes. A blacksmith wields many tools, chief amongst them are the hammer, tongs, anvil, and forge - all used harmoniously. The forge Will uses was passed down from his great-grandfather.

One of Will's "highest" achievements is a weather vane that adorns the top of the Convention & Visitors Bureau tower, one the tallest points in the city.

Some of his other self-installed creations are exhibited as far away as Antarctica.

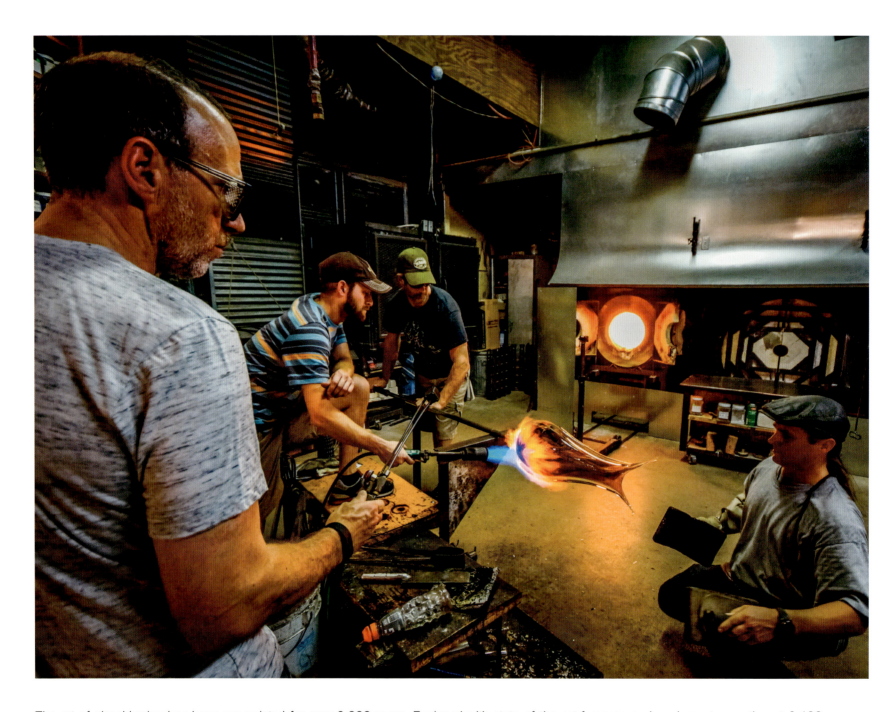

The art of glassblowing has been appreciated for over 2,000 years. Equipped with state-of-the-art furnaces and equipment operating at 2,400 degrees, Vetro Glassblowing Studio & Gallery artists transform approximately 12,000 pounds of glass each year, creating everything from ornaments and vases to sculptures and museum-worthy works of art. A thirty-person viewing area allows spectators a glimpse behind the scenes of this rare art form. Vetro is known world-wide for its creations; one masterpiece was delivered to a Saudi Arabian prince.

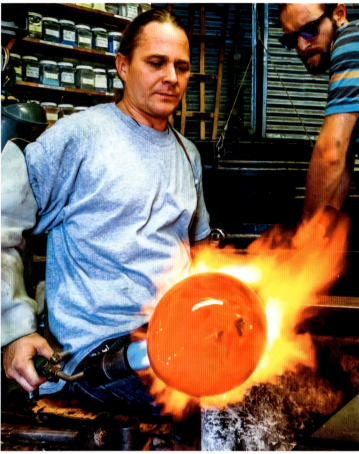

A crisp fall night is pierced by the sounds of music from a bygone era. The songs bear the static of old age, but cross the ear with a wistful familiarity. A few men resting atop the old-world box cars, sitting on the famous Grapevine railroad tracks, look as if they were plucked from a steel mill or from a skyscraper under construction at the turn of the century. The men power up their buzz-saws and the sparks start to fly. After a lengthy work shift, the leader sounds an air horn signaling a short break and the men retire to the edge of the box car to watch the events unfold below. The courtyard is lit by lights strung high overhead. Withered and oxidized trash cans are set ablaze with fire to warm the area as visitors start filing in to the annual, Glass on the Tracks. On the fringes, Blacksmith Will Frary is hard at work and an artisan glass-blower is hypnotizing the audience. The pair gives onlookers quite a show.

Jenin Gonzalez, fire breather and twirler

Glass on the Tracks attendees dressed in their finest steampunk* themed attire enjoy the feast and festivities. Fire shoots into the sky from a pyrotechnic art piece and flames dance on the water standing in the middle of the piece. Fire breathers descend on chains down the side of the train cars while devil stick (fire baton) twirlers draw crowds of people around them. Models donning glass attire strut up to their individual stages for the crowd to behold.

*Steampunk is a sci-fi cultural movement highlighting a period of the 19th century when industrial steam-powered technology dominated the country. Attire may include prospector goggles, top hats, and knee-length duster coats for the men and veils, flowing dresses, knee-high boots, and Victorian corsets for the women.

After eating and drinking their fill, attendees await the grand finale - the infamous Glass on the Tracks auction. Vetro auctions some of its finest works of art and if the secret reserve is not met on special pieces up for auction, the piece is placed in a guillotine. In an instant the blown-glass masterpiece is reduced to shards of rubble.

Aptly named, Glass on the Tracks must be experienced to be believed. Attendees travel great distances each year to participate and observe the wonder of it all.

The art of lost wax casting, raku firing, sculpture, and wheel thrown pottery are some of the many studio workshops offered by owner, Pat Bodnyk at Holder Dane Gallery & Art Studios.

The gallery is filled with an array of sculptures, paintings, fine pottery, and contemporary art jewelry.

Lost wax casting, pictured on the right, is the process by which a wax model is encased in a mold, burned out, and then cast into fine metals. Twigs, pinecones, and seashells are just a few of the organic materials this studio casts in their original form to create delicate sculptural pieces.

*One touch of nature makes
the whole world kin.*

-William Shakespeare

 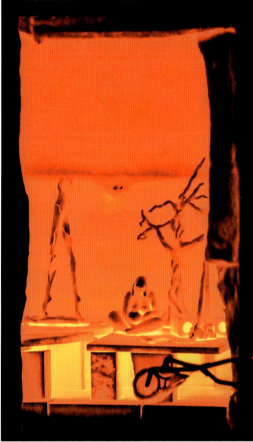 

ra·ku
noun

1. A process by which pottery is fired at a relatively low temperature and then moved while red hot into a closed container with combustible materials (such as paper or sawdust) that ignite and cause a reaction creating colors and patterns on the surface of the pottery.

Fascinating effects are achieved as the glaze melts in the firing process. It appears that ice is floating on the glowing, red-hot clay that is plunged into a flammable nest that bursts into flames, resulting in unexpected swirls of smoky colors.

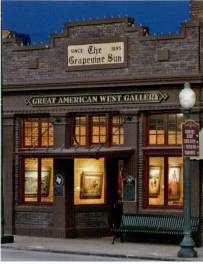

Constructed in 1897, this historic building served as a general store until 1919 when it became Tarrant County State Bank. In 1947, The Grapevine Sun newspaper moved its press here and occupied the space for 63 years. The Grapevine Sun was founded by B.R. Wall in 1895 and two years later, J.E. Keeling took ownership of the newspaper. J.E. and his family ran the business and delivered the news hot off the press for 80 years.

Now, an impressive collection of paintings and sculptures by nationally recognized Western artists fill the former newsroom. The Great American West Gallery showcases masterpieces ranging in price from $5,000 to $400,000. Paintings even fill the walls of a vault located inside the gallery. It is the original vault that served Tarrant County State Bank.

An embodiment of Grapevine's association with the arts, Sonya Terpening showcases a regularly changing collection of her most current paintings at the Great American West Gallery. Sonya has worked in the studio in her Grapevine home for 28 years and is recognized locally and nationally. Her watercolor and oil paintings can be found in museums and galleries across the United States. Sonya was the first woman to win an award for art at the prestigious Masters of the American West invitational art show at the Autry Museum in Los Angeles, CA.

Art so good it will have you seeing double.

Artists and owners of Gypsy Muse Studio, twin sisters Sharen Chatterton and Karen Rester provide a creative atmosphere for hands-on art classes and workshops.

The hippy, gypsy-themed boutique is filled to the brim with art, eclectic merchandise, and handmade artisan gifts. Immerse yourself in the good karma of Gypsy Muse, it will have you coming back for more.

Porcelain artwork, traditionally known as China painting, has been a popular pastime for thousands of years. Grapevine is fortunate to be the home of the International Porcelain Artists and Teachers (IPAT) Museum. IPAT was founded in 1958 and moved to Grapevine in 1996. The museum features an exquisite collection of painted porcelain from around the world.

Former IPAT President, Bertie Stephens, is pictured above, painting a child self-portrait on porcelain. Bertie is taught by American-Venezuelan artist Mariela Villasmil.

Aptly named, A Touch of Paris art gallery is owned by Paris native, Dominique Galleron-Johnson, and is an alluring escape for those wanting to watch or learn as Dominique wields a palette knife to create beautiful masterpieces.

The gallery offers special events and a private patio to mingle and even enjoy a cigar. Experience A Touch of Paris and a taste of the good life? Oui.

Housed in a building that's part winery tasting room, the Giddens Gallery of Fine Art includes unique and exceptional designs to enjoy, one of which is UpCycled Fine Art - art made of unwanted or normally discarded materials.

Behold the work of artists of multiple mediums who have studied with masters of their craft and sold their works internationally. One of the gallery's celebrated attractions is the artist herself; Naomi Brotherton is a 95-year-old renowned watercolor painter who pushes through Macular Degeneration to do so.

Chocolate Artist, Aaron Drew

Board Certified in Internal Medicine and practicing full time, Dr. Sue also wears the Wonka hat as the proud owner of a chocolate factory, and can verify that all-natural, dark chocolate is a healthy treat.

All recipes at Dr. Sue's Chocolate are artistically created by hand, in store. During the holiday season the kitchen generates over 250 pounds of chocolate per day.

Recipes include local and imported ingredients, the most expensive of which - piment d'espelette, a dried pepper from Provence - rings in at over $150 per pound. The most popular flavors are Cherry Pecan Bark and Hazelnut Toffee.

Patrons can sample exclusive flavors and request custom orders as well. One unique order was chocolate covered black eyed peas. That will bring you the sweet taste of good luck in the New Year!

One consumed chocolate chip can give a person enough energy to walk 150 feet. The amount of chocolate consumed at ChocolateFest could power a small city.

Americans consume 2.8 billion pounds of candy each year. Nearly half of this is chocolate. More than 13,000 visitors from all corners of the country have consumed over 231,000 samples of chocolate at Grapevine's ChocolateFest since its inception.

The annual festival benefits Travelers Aid Dallas/Fort Worth, a non-profit agency which provides aid to over 65,000 distressed travelers annually. They may have helped you or a loved one.

These perceptions of Grapevine were created by Grapevine High School artists.

The first graduating class of Grapevine High School was in 1908. One diploma was awarded.

Today, approximately 1,900 students fill the classrooms. One notable graduate is HGTV's *Fixer Upper*, Chip Gaines

Go Mustangs!

Andi Risk

Cara Kelley

Jesus Maltos

Isabel Liang

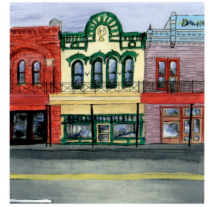
Katelyn Noble

Kaylee Galvan

SeoJung Yoon

Kelsie Baldwin

Mariam Shaphek

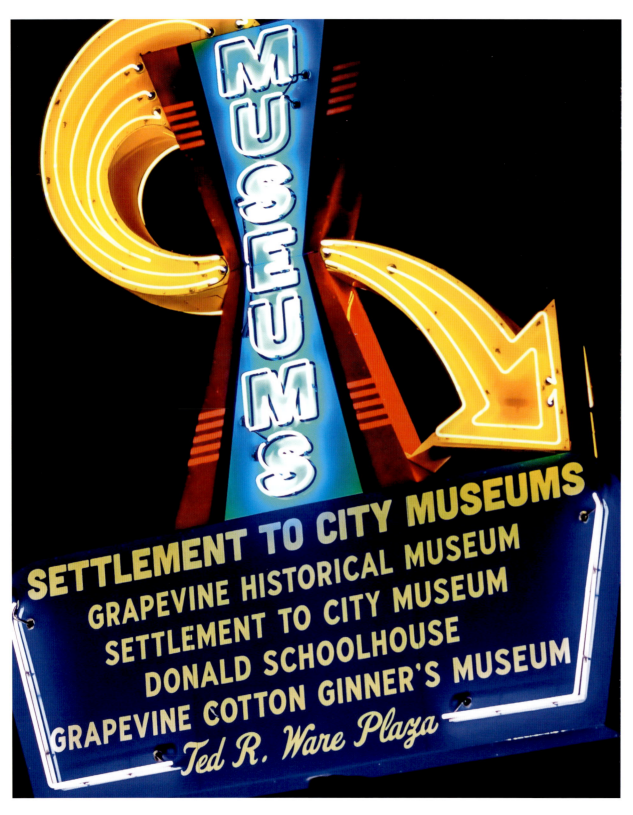

The Settlement to City Museums art deco, neon lit sign is a refurbished and restored historic sign that at one time advertised a flower shop on Main Street.

The Settlement to City Museum highlights more than 100 years of Grapevine history with a timeline of photos, stories, and artifacts. One such artifact is a working, circa 1881 Chandler & Price letterpress similar to the one used to produce The Grapevine Sun newspaper.

Located in a circa 1900 building equipped with a fully functional ringable bell on a rope, vintage desks, antique school books, and slates used the learn the 3 R's, the Donald Schoolhouse Museum portrays public education on the Grape Vine Prairie in 1900. The building was originally part of the Donald Academy located north of Denton Creek.

It's the perfect place to reminisce and share with little ones who can't imagine a world without video games, laptops, and cell phones.

After the Civil War the cotton industry was a major catalyst for growth in Grapevine. Located inside a circa 1910 house originally located on the Sidney Webb Cotton Gin property, the Cotton Ginners Museum showcases the history and industrialization of one of the world's most important crops. On display is a miniature wheel gin and spinning wheel. Museum visitors are able to follow the invention of the first cotton gin, and imagine the long grueling days of hand-picking acres of cotton and toting it in 100-pound bags.

In May of 1932, a "Tallest, Smallest and Stoutest" competition was hosted to commemorate the opening of Northwest Highway. Mayor E.E. Lowe took the prize as the tallest at 6-feet 6-inches. Nick "Uncle Nick" Pearson, 76 years of age at the time, won smallest at 40 inches and weighed in at 58 pounds. Clarence F. Millican took the award for the stoutest at 350 pounds.

"Uncle Nick" was known throughout town for tapping phone lines to listen in on phone conversations, which made him quite the storyteller. He smoked a corn cob pipe and, despite his intrusive nature, was a beloved character. His tiny coat is now on display at the Grapevine Historical Museum.

Running a marathon, selling raffle tickets, or hosting a bake sale for charitable purposes was seemingly mundane for some in the early 1900s. From the 1910s to 1960s, womanless weddings were held with pretend nuptials to raise money for churches, charitable causes, and civic organizations.

All roles, from groom and minister to bride and flower girl were portrayed by men. Gentlemen donned full makeup, wigs, bonnets, gowns, and jewelry for the ceremony. The phenomenon is rumored to have started in the South, but quickly spread across the nation. The weddings featured some of the city's most prominent male residents in comic renditions of the betrothal. Grapevine residents were amongst those that engaged in the Southern tradition.

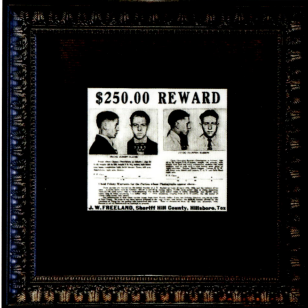

The infamous Bonnie and Clyde used the area near Denton Creek (now Grapevine Lake) to hide out and meet with friends between crime sprees. Hilton DFW Lakes, Grapevine's first full-service conference center hotel, now stands in the "hideout" area. Inside the hotel visitors will find Bonnie & Clyde's Hideout, a restaurant and bar that showcases relics of the notorious couple's wild story including wanted posters, newspaper articles, historic photographs, and even some of Bonnie's poetry.

Once upon a time…they met, they courted, they fell in love.

Friends and neighbors have followed their love story for many years, attended their wedding, and even named their first son, Patch.

Mr. and Mrs. Scarecrow, their son Patch, and Fido are community icons that have resided at Nash Farm since 2006 and dress for every occasion.

The creative genius and matchmaker responsible for introducing and caring for these love birds…Linda Ratliff.

Walk through 165,000 gallons of water in a 360-degree glass tunnel to view some of the planet's most beautiful aquatic acrobats at SEA LIFE Grapevine Aquarium.

The 240,000-gallon indoor oasis is home to more than 5,000 fresh and saltwater creatures. Sharks and seahorses are bred on-site and visitors are invited to view the seahorse nursery.

The aquarium rescues and rehabilitates sea turtles from the Animal Rehabilitation Keep (ARK) in Port Aransas, Texas. Also rescued and displayed are piranhas which were seized from a home in Texas, where it's illegal to own a piranha without a permit. Someone must have seen the culprit taking the fish for a walk.

Home to more than 2 million LEGO® bricks, LEGOLAND® is an epic adventure of miniature proportions. From amusement park style rides to a 4D cinema and earthquake tables where LEGO buildings get the ultimate test, LEGOLAND has it all pieced together.

DFW's most recognizable buildings and monuments are miniaturized in MINILAND®. Prominent skylines are displayed alongside Dallas/Fort Worth International Airport, Grapevine's Main Street, and more. There is even a miniature SEA LIFE Grapevine Aquarium and LEGOLAND inside LEGOLAND.

The number of LEGO blocks inside MINILAND is a staggering 1 million, and even more remarkable is the number of man hours necessary to construct replicas of local attractions. It took more than 452 man-hours to assemble the miniature AT&T Stadium, home of the Dallas Cowboys.

Like a beacon in the night, Grapevine Mills mall draws throngs of people to visit the numerous shops and attractions. One of the most interesting elements found inside the retail paradise is a full-size working carousel.

1.8 million square feet, 62,000 light bulbs, 2.8 million feet of electrical wire - enough to wind back and forth from Dallas to Fort Worth 17 times, and 1.4 million square feet of carpet are just a few of the mind-blowing stats that make up Grapevine Mills mall.

1.6 million hours were clocked during construction of the mall, which is equivalent to 800 years. It would take 16 people, working full-time, more than 50 years to accumulate this many hours. Thankfully, the construction crew was more than 16 strong. The gargantuan retail mecca opened in 1997. Nearly 14 million people visited the mall in the first year, generating over $300 million in sales.

Two giant wolf statues guard the entry and have kept watch over the inhabitants of Great Wolf Lodge® since its opening in 2007. The family resort is equipped with an indoor water park that is longer than 37 Olympic-size swimming pools but, amazingly, circulates only 650,000 gallons of water. This is 10,000 gallons less than just one Olympic-size pool, making it a very efficient system.

The Great Wolf Lodge® famous "tipping bucket" dumps 1,000 gallons of water every five minutes. A warning bells gives guests enough time to be ready for the excitement of the big splash.

The water park boasts 6,200 feet of water slides which is equivalent to about twenty-and-a-half times the height of the Statue of Liberty.

The times, they keep a-changin! The railroad arrived to Grapevine in 1888, and shortly thereafter brick buildings dotted Main Street replacing the wood buildings which had been the town's face for 50 years. A fair majority of the bricks used for the buildings were made by Jake Waymire, a local brick mason.

What started as a small hub of civilization, has evolved over the course of the past 172 years into a booming town with a population of nearly 50,000. Main Street is now a draw for shopping, wining, and dining of all kinds. The historic buildings are filled with popular boutiques selling vintage clothing, jewelry, unique gifts, home décor and more. Where else can you buy chic cowboy boots in a 100-year-old building? Main Street is listed on the National Register of Historic Places.

There's a seamless transition from Main Street into the bordering township neighborhood. The homes therein are kept to the highest standards. Once a year, the Grapevine Candlelight Tour of Homes offers a glimpse inside select historic homes, businesses on Main Street, and new infill houses built in historic style.

"My family owned a grocery and hardware store on Main Street when I was young. The doors were left open at all of the businesses to allow air flow. There was dust everywhere. FloorSweep was sprinkled on the floors to help with the dirt."

-Mayor William D. Tate

My Love Came Back starring Olivia de Havilland was shown at the formal opening of the Palace Theatre on November 21, 1940. It was a fitting title for what would be a tumultuous story for this iconic Grapevine attraction. The price of admission in 1940 was 10 cents for adults and 5 cents for children.

In 1973, the Palace "motion picture" Theatre closed following the showing of *Serpico* starring Al Pacino. Two years later, the Palace doors re-opened as the home of the new Grapevine Opry country music show produced by local talent, Chisai Childs. The community embraced the format change.

By 1991, however, bankruptcy threatened closure and the theatre was purchased by the Grapevine Heritage Foundation. In 1995, the love really did come back to the Palace Theatre when $5 million was raised to restore the relic to its former glory. Musician Rocky Gribble operated the Grapevine Opry and entertained fans each weekend for nearly 20 years.

The Palace Theatre now features classic movies and attendees really get into the spirit by dressing for the occasion. Moviegoers have been known to dress in *Star Wars* character garb, *Jaws* shark costumes, and *Wizard of Oz* attire. Raphael himself has even stopped by to sign autographs at a showing of *Teenage Mutant Ninja Turtles*.

When classic movies aren't on the menu, the venue hosts a variety of live entertainment. Over the years, the stage has been graced by famous musicians such as LeAnn Rimes, Miranda Lambert, Porter Wagoner, and Charlie Pride. In May 1980, country music legend Willie Nelson stopped in for a performance.

Built in 1997, Grapevine City Hall features an array of the city's past. The columns are replicas of those on the old Farmers National Bank. The arched brickwork is modeled after Willhoite's Warehouse, formerly a local public school. The 14 stars represent the Grapevine City Council along with the Planning & Zoning Commission members.

Real treasures await visitors inside City Hall. A clock used by the town's nightwatchmen is on display alongside a .35 caliber Remington rifle used by Grapevine Mayor Gordon Tate during the capture of a Bonnie and Clyde gang member after the robbery of Grapevine Home Bank in 1932.

"When I was a kid, City Council met around a card table at City Hall."

-Mayor William D. Tate

THE GRAPEVINE FARMERS MARKET MAKES SUPPORTING LOCAL FARMERS FUN AND CONVENIENT.

A SMORGASBORD OF HARVESTED NUTS, FRUITS, VEGETABLES, JAMS, JELLIES, AND MORE THAN 15 TYPES OF SALSA FILL THE SHELVES OF THE INDOOR YEAR-ROUND MARKET. EACH SUMMER, THE MARKET EXPANDS OUTDOORS AND FILLS THE GAZEBO AREA ON MAIN STREET. THE AROMA OF ROASTING HATCH GREEN CHILES LURES "FOODIES" IN LIKE MOTHS TO A FLAME.

THE GRAPEVINE MARKET, AN OPEN-AIR EUROPEAN STYLE SHOPPING EXPERIENCE ALSO SPROUTS UP EACH SUMMER ON MAIN STREET IN LIBERTY PARK. MERCHANTS CARRY LOCAL AND HAND-MADE JEWELRY, HOME DÉCOR, ANTIQUES AND MORE.

A TURQUOISE BROCHE AND A JAR OF LOCAL HONEY... A SHOPPING DELIGHT YOU NEVER KNEW YOU ALWAYS NEEDED.

Located in the heart of downtown, the Town Square Gazebo serves as a stage for festival bands, weddings, and special performances.

The pavilion was constructed in 1986, and sits on land once used as a livery stable that housed horses and carriages in the 1890s and early 1900s. In 1937, the stables were torn down and a gas station was built. The price of gasoline in 1937 was only 15 cents per gallon!

With an estimated 400 million cups enjoyed per day, the United States consumes more coffee than any other country in the world. Humans aren't the only ones indulging in the popular beverage. The oldest cat in history was served coffee every morning by her owner. According to the Guinness Book of World Records, "Creme Puff" reached 38 years and 3 days.

RE:defined Coffee House doesn't cater to senile felines, but you will find some "cool cats" enjoying hand-made drinks at this swanky establishment. The owner's brought-from-home décor and furnishings create a unique and welcoming "living room" feel which encourages caffeinated connoisseurs to share spaces and experiences.

Be cool. They've got the rhythm down pat at HipPop. Compositions include incredible flavor combinations that sizzle and satisfy the most inquisitive palate. The hip hop themed flavor combinations are the bread and butter (although not a flavor option) of this local favorite.

Only a true artisan of flavor profiles could blend sweet strawberries with earthy basil. Signature recipes also include the Busta Lime, a combination of sour lime with a bite of jalapeno and crisp mouth-watering cucumber, and 2 Lime Crew, a thirst-quenching watermelon lime mixture. These are just a few of the offerings that span menus of popsicles, shaved ice, and slushes.

It's totally cool and radically sweet.

What do you want to eat? Perhaps, the most frequently asked question at every mealtime in nearly every home. Why not try, well...everything? The Great Taste of Grapevine features more than 25 local restaurants showcasing their finest and favorite dishes, in sample form. Beer and wine bars, live music, and over 650 attendees make this dinner party one for the books (hence it's inclusion in this one).

The event has been held annually for over 20 years and is hosted by the Grapevine Chamber of Commerce Women's Division. Proceeds benefit local school supply and senior adult programs.

The Grapevine Chamber of Commerce hosts numerous events throughout the year including everything from golf tournaments to casino nights.

Established in 1952, the organization has grown to over 900 members who work together to promote business and foster economic development for the growing city of Grapevine.

Top row: Chill Sports Bar
Second row: A.J.'s On Main, Weinberger's Deli
Third row: Tommy Tamale, Esparza's Restaurante Mexicano
Bottom row: Wise Guys Pizzeria

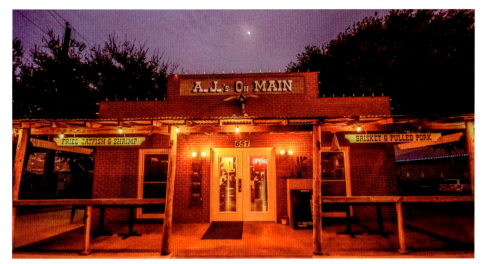

Nothing grabs a Southerner's attention quite like the aroma of barbecue on the grill. A.J.'s On Main is located near the Grapevine Vintage Railroad and is themed to match the local motif. The interior of the restaurant features train tracks winding through the dining area, painted by local artist Erika Krivda. Unique sports and Texas paraphernalia are also on display.

The outdoor smoker, producing the appetizing aromatherapy, replicates (to scale) an old steam engine. It was designed in the restaurant and took six months to build. Adorning the smoker is the badge of Darren Medlin, the only Grapevine police officer to have lost his life in the line of duty.

The proprietor, AJ, retired from the Grapevine police force in 2008 and decided instead to use his talents to serve residents delicious food. The signature sauce, mouth-watering barbecue, and unique coleslaw make this restaurant and watering hole a local favorite.

For a taste of local history, the restaurant features seven bricks cemented into the outdoor patio. These bricks were extracted from the ground under A.J.'s and belonged to the original Wallis Hotel, built in 1891.

Texas Star Dinner Theater…Where Historical Meets Hysterical®

It is anything but a typical theater. It's an exciting, interactive, comedy-infused murder mystery. The actors perform, not on a stage, but rather in the dining area amongst the tables, and often times an unsuspecting audience member will be pulled into the action. After patrons enjoy a gourmet three-course meal, they are drawn into the 1880s when cattle herds, cowboys, drifters, and gamblers could be found roaming the streets.

Originally debuting in the Fort Worth Stockyards as Lone Star Murder Mysteries, this band of bandits moved their show to Grapevine in 2004. The critically acclaimed scripts are written in-house and take a year to develop. Centered around Marshal Jim Courtright, a real-life 1880s lawman from Fort Worth, the theater provides murder mystery aficionados an intriguing challenge for their investigative skills and more hilarity than the law allows!

Care for some tea and crumpets? Bangers and mash? An enormous collection of imported British groceries, unique goodies, and pop culture gifts line the shelves at the British Emporium. There is plenty to entertain the Anglophiles as well. Royal events include Queen Elizabeth look-a-like competitions along with Royal wedding and birth celebrations. Short and stout is the name of the game for the Corgi dog shows and ugly teapot contests.

Photograph by Dean Campbell

This is not your typical restaurant; walk, row, sail, or paddle aboard. Big Daddy's Ship Store is Grapevine's only floating restaurant. Boat parking available.

This lake-side grill has been flipping some of the best burgers in Grapevine since 1997 and is one of Grapevine's best kept secrets. Local sports icons have been known to stop by and soak in the surroundings.

Did you know Texas consumes more craft beer per capita than Ireland or Germany?

Over 500,000 gallons of beer are brewed each year at Grapevine Craft Brewery, making it the 10th fastest growing brewery in the U.S. in 2014.

Each brew has been appropriately named to honor various Grapevine staples, two of which include the Monarch, a filtered American Wheat Ale reflecting the Grapevine path of the monarch butterfly, and Sir William's, an English style Brown Ale named for Grapevine's long-standing Mayor, William D. Tate.

Craft brew, live music, food trucks, trivia nights, and a table of your best friends. What more could you need?

Mayor William D. Tate, the longest serving mayor in Grapevine's history, has held the position since 1973 with the exception of one term. His father, Gordon Tate, also served as a Grapevine mayor from 1949 to 1952. Like father, like son.

The festivals provide an opportunity for Mayor William D. Tate to expand his wardrobe in an effort to educate, entertain, and promote Grapevine. The tradition is one which has lasted many years.

 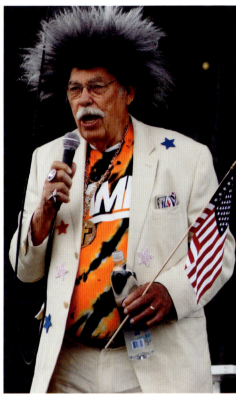  
  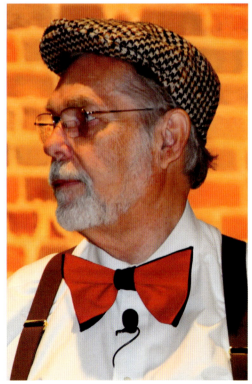 

Grapevine has joined hands across the globe in partnering with three sister cities; Parras de la Fuente, Mexico; Krems, Austria; and West Lothian, Scotland. The partners bear mutual benefits from the program's professional, educational, and cultural exchanges. Travel professionals and tourism experts in each country share their experiences and knowledge in marketing their hometowns.

Parras de la Fuente, Mexico - Population: 45,423

Parras de la Fuente, founded in 1598, translates to "Grapevines of the Fountain." The agricultural town with vast vineyards is located in northern Mexico in the state of Coahuila.

Festivities and traditions at the annual grape festival, Feria de la Uva, are very similar to those at Grapevine festivals. Some of the festivities include the dancing Matachines, a Grape Queen parade, Stomping of the Grapes, and Blessing of the Vines.

Parras is also home to the oldest winery in the Western Hemisphere, Casa Madero, which was founded in 1597. Local attractions include *Iglesia del Santo Madero*, a church located on top of an extinct volcano plug, and *San Ignacio de Loyola* Church, which was constructed in the 17th century.

Krems, Austria - Population: 23,898

Historically, the first mention of Krems dates back to the year 995. The town captivates its visitors with ancient buildings, quaint shops, family restaurants, and sidewalk coffee shops. Krems sits in the heart of vineyard country on the left bank of the Danube River, and its 1,000-year history is rich with traditions of wine making. Grapes of the highest caliber thrive in the vineyards of Krems. Classic varieties include Grüner Veltliner and Riesling.

Thousands of visitors travel to Krems each year to attend the Danube Festival, East-West Music Festival, Wachau Film Festival, and numerous other art, musical, and theatrical events.

West Lothian, Scotland - Population: 162,840

Scotland embodies rich heritage. West Lothian is no exception and is much more than the sound of bagpipes and traditional folklore dance. West Lothian is known for Linlithgow Palace, birth place of Mary, Queen of Scots and the annual Riding of the Linlithgow Marches.

Much like Grapevine, West Lothian retains its sense of small town charm and rich history. The King's Fountain, located in the Palace courtyard, dates back to 1537 and is Scotland's oldest surviving fountain.

Grapevine and West Lothian have developed an education-based relationship that has benefitted students in both locations. Golf, culinary, band, and music exchange students have reaped the advantages of travel abroad.

Don Bigbie and friend Paul W. McCallum, Executive Director of the Grapevine Convention & Visitors Bureau for nearly 30 years, took the occasional road trip to Montague, Texas where they would look in on the local grapes and gaze at the spectacular roadside windmill collection.

The pair envisioned returning windmills to Grapevine. They enlisted the help of Eddie Fenoglio, owner of Custom Water Company, who had 25 years of experience installing and maintaining windmills. The trio brought the vision to life and some of those windmills can now be found throughout Grapevine. For these strong-willed men, the task was just a breeze. Pun intended.

Roadside windmills in Montague, Texas

Don Bigbie
1945-2015

A city, like anything great, is only as alluring and extraordinary as the people who nurture it. Entrepreneur, world traveler, wine maker, civic leader, superb story-teller, and often referred to as the "Cowboy of Wine Making," Don will always be synonymous with the success of Grapevine's wine industry.

TO EVERY THING
THERE IS A SEASON,
AND A TIME
TO EVERY PURPOSE
UNDER THE HEAVEN.

ECCLESIASTES 3:1

Each Christmas season is kicked off with the Carol of Lights. A fireworks display, Victorian carolers, and state-of-the-art performances accompany the Mayor's flipping of a switch that simultaneously illuminates the town Christmas tree and all of Main Street with over one million twinkling lights.

Grapevine is known as the Christmas Capital of Texas®, with over 1,400 events in 40-plus days. One of the most popular events is a magical journey to the North Pole. Children and their families, dressed in their finest pajamas, hop aboard the North Pole Express® train in hopes of catching a glimpse of the Jolly Old St. Nick.

> "The Methodist Church had a big Christmas dinner each year. The tree was lit and everyone got a wrapped gift to open. Each family also received a box of fruit; I distinctly remember the aroma of the fresh fruit, it smelled so good."
>
> -Mayor William D. Tate

Do you recall the most famous reindeer of all?

Rudolph the Red-Nosed Reindeer was born more than one hundred years after his flying counterparts. In 1939, a copywriter for Montgomery Ward department store, Robert L. May, wrote a Christmas-themed story about Rudolph to bring traffic to the store, and the plan worked. Montgomery Ward sold 2.5 million copies of the story that year. *Rudolph the Red-Nosed Reindeer* has since been translated into 25 a languages and made into numerous movies, books, and other products.

Rudolph might not be in attendance, but some of his descendants have been known to make an appearance at Grapevine's Carol of Lights. Live reindeer, Mrs. Claus, and Santa's turn-of-the-century sleigh are all a part of the festivities.

It's true, everything is bigger in Texas.

Grapevine's Christmas décor is no exception. These larger-than-life fiberglass ornaments, the largest measuring at a glorious 6 feet tall, are scattered throughout the town during the Christmas season. We're gonna need a bigger tree!

A Christmas spin on an old classic...sneak a kiss under the dangling Viscum album shrub, also known as Mistletoe, for a mere 25 cents, a real bargain.

The legend of Santa Claus can be traced back hundreds of years. Monk St. Nicholas for whom Santa is believed to be named, was born sometime around 280 A.D. St. Nicholas gave away all of his inherited wealth and traveled the countryside helping the poor and sick.

St. Nicholas' nickname was Sinterklaas, an abbreviation of the Dutch translation of Saint Nicholas. The nickname Sinterklaas evolved to become Santa Claus.

Santa Claus is not the only gift-giving character that visits homes during Christmastime. Variations of the jolly old elf can be found around the world.

In Scandinavia, Jultomten rides on a sleigh, led by goats, to every home on Christmas Eve.

Before going to bed, French children place their shoes by the fireplace and fill them with carrots and treats for Père Noël's donkey, Gui. If the child has been good, presents are left in the shoes, in place of the carrots.

In Russia, an elderly woman named Babouschka has been known to leave presents on the bedside tables of sleeping youngsters.

The Italian gift giver is a kind witch on a broomstick, La Befana, who comes down the chimney to fill stockings with toys and goodies.

In England, Father Christmas visits each home on Christmas Eve to fill children's stockings with holiday treats. He also visits the British Emporium in Grapevine each Christmas season.

Kris Kringle, St. Nick, Santa...
No matter what you call him, he can be found throughout the city of Grapevine, sometimes in strange and unexpected places. One such location is underwater at SEA LIFE Grapevine Aquarium swimming amongst the fish, sharks and stingrays in a 165,000-gallon tank. That might make for some soggy stockings.

Kaleidoscopes of monarch butterflies pass through Grapevine annually in their migration from Canada to Mexico. This magical event brings local residents out of their cocoons as well. Butterfly Flutterby is an annual celebration of the winged insects and their incredible journey. For nearly 20 years, adults, children, and even dogs have swarmed the street in parade form to showcase their best monarch garb.

At the end of the parade, over 700 butterflies are individually released by the youngsters and sent off to join their companions as they continue on the great migration.

Monarch butterflies are considered the "king" of the butterflies, hence the name monarch.

Fireworks are a spectacular and traditional way to celebrate the freedom and independence of this great nation. For many years Grapevine has also used fireworks to celebrate the end of the work week during summer months.

On February 20, 1973, Ordinance No. 73-08 ended a pyrotechnic prohibition and allowed the public display of fireworks; 35 short years later, Friday Night Fireworks began.

Passengers aboard Grapevine Vintage Railroad may be in for an Old West surprise. In the dog days of summer, bandits clad in spurs and chaps come aboard to bamboozle and swindle ya out o' yer spending money, sort of. Armed with blank six-shooters, the make-believe marauders board the train and hand out "loot" before being chased through the train cars by the marshal.

Legend has it that in years past, at the end of October, people have seen a headless horseman attempting the same heist.

A full moon is commonly associated with Halloween. It is often the glowing light in horror movies, and images of witches flying across a full moon are often used for Halloween decor. Oddly enough, an October 31st full moon is extremely rare; in fact the next full moon on Halloween will not occur until 2020. The most recent occurrences were 2001 and 1955. With this in mind, there's no need to worry about werewolves at GrapeYard. Zombies on the other hand, are lurking about and hungry for brains.

Grapevine's annual Halloween festival, GrapeYard, brings families and friends out for a leisurely evening of festival food, live entertainment, singing pumpkins, hayrides, and zombie paint ball. As the evening progresses, courageous souls are dared to complete the Aftermath, a half-mile haunted trail through the wooded darkness of Meadowmere Park. A bold few traverse various terrains evading zombies in search of survivors. Don't count on a full moon to light the path.

Makeup Artist - Amanda Moseley

As the moon moves through the clouds and the wind begins to howl, a figure stumbles out of a local winery with a haunting look on its face and red liquid stains on the front of its shirt. The beginning of a scary movie? No, it's what you might see the night of Grapevine's Hallo-Wine Trail. Attendees dress in their Halloween best and tour the city's wineries with other guys, gals, ghouls, and goblins in creepy costumes and maleficent makeup. The big kids are the ones trick-or-treating this chilling evening.

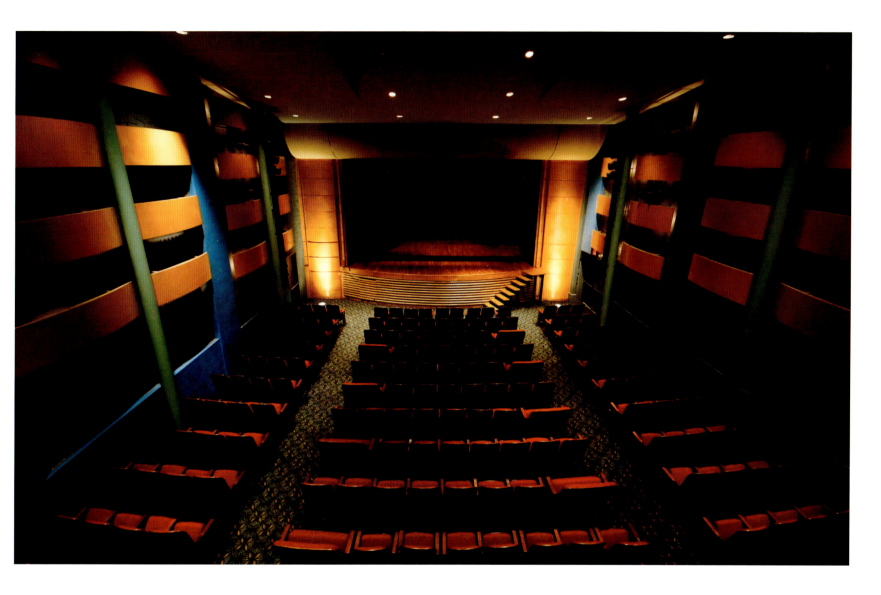

Theatres are notorious for superstitions. According to those who follow these urban legends, a light should be left on around the clock to ward off ghosts, and theatres should be empty at least one night per week to allow ghosts privacy. Perhaps the strangest superstition involves audience members picking flowers from local graveyards to give to show directors as an offering of good luck. Apparently, the afterlife is filled with actors that never got their big break.

The Palace Arts Center is composed of the Palace Theatre built in 1940, and the Lancaster Theatre, which was once Buckner Grocery in the 1930s. Both theatres are rumored to have picked up a few lingering stage-loving spirits over the years. Late nights after live shows and productions, shadows of people have been seen moving through interior doorways when only one staff member was in the building and all exterior doors were locked.

Movie posters were once displayed on the front windows in plexiglass holders which were hooked and suction cupped to the windows. On occasion, during the darkest hours of the night when all employees had left except for the manager, the top left suction cups of all seven posters would mysteriously come unhooked and leave the posters hanging in uniform angles from the right side.

In the early years of the city, a nightwatchman walked the streets and checked the doors of all the businesses to ensure they had been locked. Ghosts of nightwatchmen have been heard rattling the theatre doors late at night as they continue their work from beyond the grave.

Built in 1875, this historic homestead was originally owned by Dr. William E. Dorris, a family physician. His family lived in the dwelling, where he also practiced medicine, for only one year. The Brock family later lived in the small two bedroom house and raised a family of 12. Ownership changed multiple times over the years until Don Bigbie purchased the home and opened Cross Timbers Winery.

Cross Timbers is famous for its wine and beautiful scenic surroundings and infamous for the numerous hauntings. Recognized paranormal societies and "ghost hunters" have visited the winery to experience or debunk the hauntings; all experienced something strange and unexplainable. The reports indicated a presence of 12 male ghosts in the barn and one female ghost in the main house.

One of the most obvious recurring incidents is in the *Patti Weatherman* room. The storage cabinets were built close to the ceiling - too high to make retrieving anything from them convenient. Even with their height, the cabinets are all repeatedly opened in the same configuration; no one knows who is responsible for opening them.

One evening, a couple went into Cross Timbers for a wine tasting and the husband visited the *Patti Weatherman* room, one of the tasting areas. Later, he told the staff he had a conversation with an apparition of a woman whose name started with the letter "P". He added that the figure had a gray cloud in front of her. Patti Weatherman, a previous owner for whom the room was named, had passed away with lung cancer. Rumor has it, after Patti's passing her daughters stopped by one day but fled after only 25 minutes, claiming to feel their mother's presence still in the house, patting their head and brushing up against their cheeks. They even smelled her perfume.

On another occasion, a beach-themed party was held in the barn and ran a bit late. When the catering manager arrived the next morning to clean up, he opened the barn door and was suddenly hit in the face by a flying beach ball. He didn't return to the barn without a trusty chaperone. Many employees over the years have been reluctant to enter the barn alone. Indistinct voices and music have been heard, as well as what sounds like chairs being dragged on the floor above. The sound of falling objects is also common, although nothing has actually been moved or dropped in the room.

An unnerving and inexplicable incident occurred one morning around 7 a.m. as a strange woman was wandering around the property. The owner called a staff member to inquire whether she had an appointment to show the venue for an event, assuming the wandering woman was a client. The employee checked her calendar and confirmed her first appointment was not until noon.

The owner yelled, "Ma'am, excuse me, ma'am can I help you?"
The employee then heard a gasp and, "I'll have to call you back." The phone was hung up.

Assuming everything was fine, the employee did not check back for a few hours. When she called to check in around 10 a.m., the owner was out on the back porch having a beer.

"Having a beer at 10 a.m.?" she asked.
"That woman walking around outside this morning, as I walked toward her, she never acknowledged me, but she walked into the barn," he uttered.

"What was she doing in the barn?" was the obvious question.
"I don't know; I left. She walked into the barn on the side where there isn't a door."

Cross Timbers Winery

Patti Weatherman room

Unidentifiable object captured on exterior surveillance cameras

cal·a·boose
noun

1. Spanish derivative of Calabozo
2. English translation: dungeon or prison

Built in 1914, this 8' x 10' x 8' street-side calaboose was once used to detain drunks and lawbreakers. Since the nightwatchman was also a dog catcher, the first prisoner was rumored to be a dog. Perhaps Fido had one too many cocktails.

If you're attempting to face your claustrophobia or phasmophobia (fear of ghosts), the calaboose also serves as a popular photo op for the fearless. Many whom have gone inside after dark say the chains rattle and the door moves without being touched by any visible being.

One of the most notorious haunts is the Dorris House, built by physician and surgeon, Dr. Thomas Benton Dorris, around 1896. The Dorris family owned the home for 83 years. Legend has it, Mrs. Dorris was renowned for her cooking and in the mid to late 1900s, the home was sought for rental by newlyweds in hopes the new bride would learn how to cook through "spiritual guidance."

Dr. Dorris

Dr. Dorris, in his carriage, making a house call to a Grapevine patient, circa 1912

Around 1998, the Dorris House invited new spirits when it opened its doors as a funeral home. One evening during renovations, the funeral director, working on the third floor, heard a dial tone emitting from the first floor. He went down the spiral staircase expecting to find workers who had bumped the phone, but found no one. After this occurred three or four more times he got spooked and left for the evening.

An African Gray parrot named Sandy lived in the funeral home. Out of the blue and without prompt, the parrot started saying, "Hello, Mrs. Dorris." Evidently someone also had an affinity for the parrot; "I LOVE SANDY" randomly appeared and remains in the concrete on the front porch as if it were written with a finger when the concrete was originally poured. And, strangely enough, small toy soldier figurines would often appear in the most random, odd places. The funeral director would throw them away only to find them reappear on top of ceiling fan blades, door mouldings, etc.

The Victorian style home, with its six original fireplaces, is now a cutting-edge hair and nail salon, Renata Salon & Day Spa, where some believe a spirit still makes its presence known. The doorbell often rings, and no one is there. The wiring has been replaced several times, but the bell still chimes.

Someone or something appears to have a loathing for red nail polish. When the salon first opened, shattered bottles of red polish would be found on the floor in the mornings as if they had been thrown across the room. Rugs were often laid out on the floors to cover the stains and would be found rolled up in the morning. The owners eventually had to replace the stained flooring.

Renata Salon & Day Spa

A unique attraction sits smack dab in the middle of Main Street next to J.E. Foust & Son Funeral Home.

An antique hearse, purchased by the Foust family around 1904, is parked in a large glass case and accompanied by a display of antiquated embalming equipment.

Among the relics are embalming fluid injectors, syringes, wicker coffins, operating scissors, drain tube hoses, and embalming tables.

Stopping to smell the roses is good advice, even in the afterlife.

City Florist is filled with throngs of beautiful, sweet-smelling bouquets and floral arrangements. Perhaps it is these blossoms that attract the attention of nearby wandering spirits. The shop occupies a retail space originally built in 1946 and is the subject of many ghostly tales.

One such recurring incident involves a block-letter sign that reads "Fresh Flowers." The employees often arrive in the morning to find one of the blocks flipped upside down without having been touched by any living being.

On more than one occasion, employees have arrived in the morning to find merchandise on an interior shelved wall, along with supplies in an adjoining storage room, to be strewn about the floor. There is never a sign of theft or forced entry. Are miniature earthquakes to blame, perhaps, or might they have entered the *Twilight Zone*?

One afternoon, employees suddenly heard sounds of mariachi music coming from an unknown source in the floral arranging area. Upon further investigation, the music was discovered to be coming from a radio tucked under a shelf that the employees did not know existed. Apparently the spirits were in the mood for a fiesta!

To some, the most perplexing occurrence takes place in the back room where floral arrangements are prepared. On multiple occasions, and in plain sight, an industrial-style water sprayer has detached from the wall and forcefully sprayed water without the help of anyone near it. This phenomenon has even been captured on video by the shop owner and viewed by many skeptics.

The black and white photograph to the left was found inside the storage closet when City Florist acquired the space.

REFERENCES

Information provided by included businesses and attractions, City of Grapevine, Grapevine Chamber of Commerce, Grapevine Convention & Visitors Bureau, Grapevine Historical Society, Grapevine Masonic Lodge, Fort Worth Convention & Visitors Bureau, and:

10Best: Urban campgrounds
www.usatoday.com/story/travel/destinations/10greatplaces/2014/08/07/urban-campgrounds

12 Facts About Chocolate That Will Blow Your Mind!
www.cosmopolitan.in/life/news/a3424/things-you-never-knew-about-chocolate

America's Coffee Obsession: Fun Facts That Prove We're Hooked
www.huffingtonpost.com/2011/09/29/americas-coffee-obsession

American Veterans Own 9 Percent of U.S. Firms
www.sba.gov/advocacy/american-veterans-own-9-percent-us-firms

The Chocolate Store.com
www.thechocolatestore.com/candyfacts

Craft Beer U.S. Market Review
www.brewersassociation.org/wp-content/uploads/2015/03
IRI_2014CraftBeerReview.pdf

David L. Phelps, Phelps Sculpture Studio
www.phelpssculpture.com/pastoraldreamer

Grapevine Convention & Visitors Bureau
www.GrapevineTexasUSA.com

Guinness World Records: Oldest Cat Ever
www.guinnessworldrecords.com/world-records/oldest-cat-ever

Gulf Coast and Gulf Coast Native Sheep
www.livestockconservancy.org/index.php/heritage/internal/gulf-coast

How Lincoln's Assassination Launched the Funeral Industry
www.smithsonianmag.com/smart-news/how-lincolns-assassination-launched-the-funeral-industry

How Tall is The Statue Of Liberty?
www.howtallisthestatueofliberty.org

How Texas Saved the French Wine Industry
www.freerepublic.com/focus/news/861474/posts

Halloween's Full Moon Will Be The First Since 1955
www.usatoday30.usatoday.com/weather/news/2001/2001-10-31-halloween-fullmoon.htm

Manchester United Becomes First Team Valued At $3 Billion
www.forbes.com/sites/mikeozanian/2013/01/27/manchester-united-becomes-first-team-valued-at-3-billion

Munson, Thomas Volney
www.tshaonline.org/handbook/online/articles/fmu08

Santa Claus
www.history.com/topics/christmas/santa-claus

Texas Wine and Grape Growers Association
www.txwines.org

Texas Wine & Trail Magazine Vineyards and Associations
www.texaswineandtrail.com/vineyards-associations

When 'Womanless Weddings' Were Trendy
www.npr.org/sections/npr-history-dept/2015/06/16/413633022/when-womanless-weddings-were-trendy

Data, citations, and facts are current and accurate at the time of printing, March 2016.

Editing assistance provided by Sallie Andrews and Lindsey Fortin.

PHOTO CREDITS

Principal Photographer - Kristi Reese, Kristi Reese Photography

Thank you to the individuals and businesses listed below for providing photos.

Unless otherwise identified below, historic photos provided by the Grapevine Convention & Visitors Bureau and Grapevine Historical Society.

page 9 - Bermuda Gold & Silver (left 2 photos)

page 10 - Bermuda Gold & Silver

page 12 - Lonesome Dove Baptist Church

page 15 - Grapevine Convention & Visitors Bureau

page 17 - Pat Stinson (bottom photos)

page 24 - Grapevine Convention & Visitors Bureau (bottom photo)

page 28 - Grapevine Convention & Visitors Bureau

page 32 - Esparza's Restaurante Mexicano

page 34 - Good Things for All Seasons

page 38 - Fort Worth Convention & Visitors Bureau (bottom photo)

page 52 - Grapevine Masonic Lodge (bottom photo)

page 54 - Mark Pavlovich

page 59, 60, 65 - Grapevine Convention & Visitors Bureau

page 63 - Grapevine Convention & Visitors Bureau (top illustration)

page 85 - Great American West Gallery (top right photo)

page 91 - Dr. Sue's Chocolate (bottom right photo)

page 92 - Grapevine Convention & Visitors Bureau

page 93, 94 - Art provided by Grapevine High School Art Students

page 95 - Grapevine Convention & Visitors Bureau (top right photo)

page 99 - City of Grapevine

page 102 - Linda Ratliff

page 107, 108 - Great Wolf Lodge®
Great Wolf Lodge® is the registered trademark of GWR IP LLC, a Delaware limited liability company and member of the Great Wolf Resorts family of companies.

page 121 - Dean Campbell

page 123, 124, 125 - Grapevine Convention & Visitors Bureau

page 128 - Ashley Anderson (bottom photo)
Custom Water Company (top photo)

page 130 - Grapevine Convention & Visitors Bureau

page 133 - British Emporium

page 134 - Grapevine Convention & Visitors Bureau

page 138 - Lagniappe Productions

page 140 - Makeup artist - Amanda Moseley

page 151 - City Florist (bottom right photo)

For a list of retailers or to purchase this book online, visit www.GrapevineTexasJourney.com or www.KristiReesePhotography.com